JOHN
LENNON

POCKET
GIANTS

JOHN LENNON

POCKET
GIANTS

ROBERT
WEBB

For Kathy, Barney and Arthur – all you need is love

Cover image © Getty Images

First published 2016

The History Press
The Mill, Brimscombe Port
Stroud, Gloucestershire, GL5 2QG
www.thehistorypress.co.uk

© Robert Webb, 2016

The right of Robert Webb to be identified as the Author
of this work has been asserted in accordance with the
Copyright, Designs and Patents Act 1988.

British Library Cataloguing in Publication Data.
A catalogue record for this book is available from the British Library.

ISBN 978 0 7509 6233 9

Typesetting and origination by The History Press
Printed and bound in Malta, by Melita Press.

Contents

Introduction – A Giant of Popular Music

Life is what happens to you, while you're busy making other plans.

John Lennon
('Beautiful Boy [Darling Boy]')

I first became aware of John Lennon when my father brought home a plastic toy guitar. On it were etched the faces and signatures of the four Beatles. They grinned out from behind the multi-coloured nylon strings that soon snapped, rendering it useless as a musical instrument. The cadence of 'John, Paul, George and Ringo' was soon a familiar one to me. It was always 'John' first: he must have been the leader. I was now able to put faces to the records I had heard on the radio, songs that by 1964 were unavoidable to anyone with ears. I'd like to say that a John Lennon song was my favourite back then, but actually it was 'All My Loving', a brisk, walking blues by his bandmate Paul McCartney; the co-written 'I Want to Hold Your Hand' was a close second though.

By the seventies I was old enough to buy my own records and, although to begin with I knew McCartney's output better, thanks to my cousin who bought everything and played it whenever we met, I was increasingly drawn to Lennon as the more controversial, and thus interesting, of the two ex-Beatles. The first of his solo albums I heard was *Mind Games*, the 1973 release which appeared to promote a 'conceptual country' Lennon called Nutopia. One track was the 'Nutopian International Anthem': three seconds of silence. That the dead space between tracks could also have titles was at least original. Elsewhere *Mind Games* was a fine little album, I thought – 'rock at different speeds', as Lennon put it.[1]

The more I listened to Lennon, the more intrigued I was. His music wasn't always great and it varied enormously, from surreal pop, banner-waving anthems and gut-wrenching diatribes, to saccharine love songs and avant-garde. As the seventies unfolded into progressive rock, new wave and electronica, Lennon withdrew into fifties rock 'n' roll.

Still, you knew that whatever form the music came in, Lennon meant it from the heart. So when I awoke on the morning of 9 December 1980 and heard back-to-back John Lennon songs on the radio, one after the other, punctuated by breaking news that he had been murdered in New York by a crazed fan, I was genuinely grief-stricken. Somehow, Lennon's assassination meant more than just the passing of a musician, however famous he was. I kept thinking of the W.H. Auden line, written for W.B. Yeats, 'What instruments we have agree/The day of his death was a dark cold day'.

As I discovered more about his backstage life – his early days, his time with the Beatles, his later years with (and without) Yoko Ono – he became a harder man to like as a person. Behind the scenes Lennon could be a monstrous egoist, cruel and selfish; but he knew this and worked out why, and addressed it as best a man of his generation and upbringing could. And sometimes he got it wrong. Over the years, this process of self-analysis was all too visible and audible. He made sure we were within earshot when he told Yoko, cloyingly so at times, how much he loved her. When he sat in bed with his new wife, naked and angry and in love, demanding that peace be given a chance, he did so with the world watching.

Lennon was one of the giants of the twentieth century. He dazzled us in the sixties and early seventies with brilliant, era-defining songs that will endure long after we are forgotten. He could have left it at that; but he also chose to speak out for what he believed in. He was an idealist and a dreamer who stood by his conviction that the world could – and should – be a better place. We forget that we only use the phrases 'all you need is love' and 'give peace a chance' because Lennon did.

1

'Who am I Supposed to Be?' – Childhood

I was hip in kindergarten. I was different from others. I was different all my life.

John Lennon
(in Sheff, *All We Are Saying*, p.156)

John Lennon will forever be associated with the city of Liverpool. It was where he lived for more than half of his relatively short life, where he drew his first breath, took his first steps and where he met his first loves. And the city, in turn, loved him back. In the 1960s, Lennon and the Beatles transformed the bustling, workaday Lancashire port into one of the most famous cities on the planet.

Between the wars Liverpool was thriving. It boasted over 7 miles of docks and a prosperous middle class, comfortable on the profits of maritime trade. The Stanley family lived in one the smartest residential areas, under the shadow of the city's imposing Anglican cathedral.

George Stanley was a sailor turned respectable insurance investigator; his five daughters were anything but conventional. The Stanley sisters grew into a domineering, headstrong quintet. Mary, known to the family as Mimi, was the eldest. Then there was Julia, occasionally known as Judy. She was, according to her daughter Julia Baird, the most unusual and unpredictable of them all, often cast in later histories – somewhat inaccurately, as Baird has shown in her own book – as a frivolous, flirtatious woman.

It was the musically intrepid Julia who would in later years show her young son his first chords on the guitar. But before that, in 1938, she married a roving seaman, Alfred Lennon, the son of an Irish clerk and one-time music-hall entertainer. 'That Alf Lennon'[2] was immediately unpopular with the Stanley family and none of Julia's sisters attended their register office wedding. Alf later claimed they married just for a laugh and that he took his bride to the cinema for their honeymoon. He was a mercurial character, establishing the pattern for the marriage by sailing for the West Indies within a week of the wedding, as a ship's steward on board one of the luxury liners that plied the Atlantic.

Julia stayed at home, receiving visits from her husband whenever he was in the country. He was on shore leave at Christmas 1939, when Julia fell pregnant. The couple's son was born at around 6.30 p.m. the following 9 October at Oxford Street Maternity Hospital. He was named John after his paternal grandfather. Liverpool, an obvious target for German bombers, had borne the brunt of aerial attacks that week. As a patriotic gesture Julia added a middle name borrowed from Britain's redoubtable new prime minister.

John Winston Lennon spent his early years at the Stanley family home in Newcastle Road, at No. 9 (a digit that would recur throughout Lennon's life, from the date of his birth to the day he died). The house was not far from the orphanage where Alf himself had grown up. John's errant father was proving to be as unreliable as the other Stanley sisters feared he would, his frequent maritime jaunts putting further strain on his and Julia's stuttering marriage.

When Julia met another man, John 'Bobby' Dykins, her sister Mimi – now, with the death of their mother, the matriarch of the family – was aghast. Julia was still married to Alf and her new home with Dykins – a small flat in the Gateacre district – was, in Mimi's emphatic opinion, an unsuitable place to raise the toddler. Mimi demanded that John be handed over to her as Julia was no longer a fit mother. When Liverpool Social Services discovered that the 5-year-old didn't even have his own bed, let alone a bedroom, they ruled in favour of the eldest sister and John was moved across town to Mimi's semi-detached house, 'Mendips', at No. 251 Menlove Avenue. Mimi and her husband George Smith, childless themselves, welcomed John into their home and for the first time the youngster began to enjoy something of a settled childhood in the quiet suburb of Woolton.

When word reached Alf Lennon – always one to turn up like a bad penny, as the Stanleys would put it – the generally absent father invited John to spend some time with him at the seaside. Julia tracked the pair down to a boarding house in Blackpool. 'She'd now got a nice little home and decided she wanted him,'[3] Alf later recalled. Alf planned to take John with him to New Zealand and, he claimed, asked Julia to accompany them. She refused. They turned to John and asked him to choose. The boy was faced with a grave choice, the outcome of which would inevitably alter the course of his life: New Zealand with his father, or back to Liverpool with Julia. Initially, it looked as if Alf's gamble had paid off. Without a moment's hesitation, according to Alf, John turned to his father. Julia asked him once more and again he replied, 'Daddy'. However when Julia rose to leave, dabbing her eyes, John ran to her. Easily resigned to the situation, Alf Lennon wouldn't see his son again until the whole world knew his name.

John returned to Mendips and life with Aunt Mimi, now more determined than ever to ensure her young nephew was raised in a secure environment. He was encouraged by Mimi to read classics such as *Just William*, *Alice's Adventures in Wonderland* and *The Wind in the Willows*. They sparked his imagination and John soon began scribbling verse and stories in his own notebooks, as well as compiling scrapbooks of cartoons and cuttings from magazines.

From 1951, increasingly he would spend time at the house his mother now shared with Bobby Dykins, a couple of miles across town. Julia loved spurring on her son's artistic endeavours and introduced him to a world of music unheard in Mimi's strait-laced household. They would jive around the lounge to Elvis Presley hits and it was Julia who later purchased John's first Teddy Boy clothes: a coloured shirt, drainpipe jeans and coat. These were carefree days for Lennon, punctuated only by the unexpected death of Mimi's husband George in 1955. John was devastated at the loss of his father figure.

At Quarry Bank High School, Lennon's approach to learning was characterised by a rebellious spirit. His 1956 school report was littered with 'could do better' and 'lacks effort'. 'He has many of the wrong ambitions and his energy is too often misplaced',[4] concluded his head teacher. Chief amongst his distractions was the latest youth craze to sweep the country: skiffle, which involved strumming acoustic guitars and plucking tea-chest basses to the percussive rhythm of scraped washboards. It was Britain's first do-it-yourself music; the only real instrument you needed was a guitar. Lennon ordered an acoustic model by mail order and Julia allowed it to be delivered to her address, rather than to his disapproving Aunt Mimi.

Ownership of a guitar was something of a coup for the ambitiously hip Lennon and in the late summer of 1956, he formed his own skiffle band, the Quarrymen, the name derived from a line in the Quarry Bank School song. The group's repertoire comprised versions of songs made famous by Lonnie Donegan, Lead Belly, Hank Williams and other musical heroes. They landed their first gig in autumn 1956 at the local church hall, and more soon followed.

By the end of his last year at high school John had converted the Quarrymen from an accomplished but run-of-the-mill skiffle outfit into a would-be rock 'n' roll band. This was inspired in part by a trip to the cinema. *The Girl Can't Help It* was *the* influential movie of the day, starring Jayne Mansfield and showcasing the 'teen' sound of Little Richard, Gene Vincent, Eddie Cochran and others. Its screening at the city's Scala Cinema in the summer of 1957 marked a pivotal moment in the development of Liverpool's musical youth. Lennon had heard the future.

Another cinema-goer who loved rock 'n' roll, and had even learned to play some of the songs by listening to Radio Luxembourg's evening broadcasts and patiently working out the chords, was a lad from neighbouring Allerton: Paul McCartney.

2

'When You're Crippled Inside' – Quarryman

That's the music that brought me from the provinces of England to the world ... I don't know where we'd have been without rock 'n' roll and I really love it.

John Lennon
(*Beatles Anthology*, p.11)

Newspapers on the morning of Saturday, 6 July 1957 bore headlines about American nuclear testing, Australian spin bowlers and Commonwealth summits. Rather prophetically, perhaps, *The Times* also reported that day on an infestation of beetles discovered in a cargo of Spanish onions unloaded at Liverpool docks.

On a day that would change their lives forever, two Liverpool teenagers were heading for Woolton's annual 'village' fete at St Peter's church. At Mendips, 16-year-old John was greasing back his hair and choosing his clothes carefully: black drainpipe jeans, check shirt. The heavy horn-rimmed glasses he usually wore to correct his poor eyesight would have to be left behind. This was a big day: the Quarrymen had a gig. They'd be riding to the fete on the back of one of the processional trucks, then playing at the event itself. Aunt Mimi, unaware that her nephew was even in a band, would be there.

Elsewhere, Paul McCartney, two weeks over the age of 15, was twanging on his Zenith guitar at the house he shared with his father and young brother. Music filled the McCartney household: his father Jim once led his own group, Jim Mac's Jazz Band, and pre-war American ballads and jazz numbers were as familiar as nursery rhymes to the young Paul. But it was the raw power of rock 'n' roll which now captivated the schoolboy's attention. In 1956 he had seen Lonnie Donegan at the Liverpool Empire and by the following year was proficient enough to work out the chords to several of his heroes' hits. Amongst his idols was Eddie Cochran.

Paul's school friend Ivan Vaughan had a garden which backed onto Mendips and Vaughan – 'Ivy' to Lennon and his friends – was one of the Woolton gang. He was well aware of both John's and Paul's interest in rock 'n' roll and suggested Paul come along to the fete to see the Quarrymen and maybe meet some girls. Paul knew John by sight but the two had never spoken. After struggling to stay upright on the float as it swayed through Woolton, the Quarrymen – John Lennon (vocals, guitar), Eric Griffiths (guitar), Colin Hanton (drums), Rod Davis (banjo), Pete Shotton (washboard) and Len Garry (tea-chest bass) – reached St Peter's for their late afternoon performance, on a makeshift stage behind the church.

When Paul and Ivan arrived, the band were running through a version of the Del-Vikings' hit 'Come Go With Me'. John was singing the wrong words, Paul noticed. 'He was filling in with blues lines,' recalled McCartney. 'I thought that was good and he was singing well … I quite liked them.'[5] Other cover versions the Quarrymen performed that sun-dappled afternoon included Lonnie Donegan's 'Puttin' on the Style', Gene Vincent's 'Be-Bop-a-Lula' and Elvis Presley's 'Baby, Let's Play House'.

The Quarrymen finished and made their way over to the church hall to set up for an evening session that would effectively close the fete. Paul and Ivy followed, and in the hall Vaughan introduced him to John. This was the meeting that changed the future of popular music.

Paul, eighteen months John's junior, showed Lennon how to tune his guitar properly and used it to sing Cochran's 'Twenty Flight Rock', 'Be-Bop-a-Lula' and a Little Richard medley. He then pounded out a version of Jerry Lee Lewis's 'A Whole Lot of Shakin' on the backstage piano. Whether or not it was thought of at the time as an audition, his obvious musicianship for one so young made him irresistible to John. Paul was invited to become a Quarryman in October 1957.

Lennon, meanwhile, was reaching the end of his schooling at Quarry Bank. Although obviously an intelligent pupil, the schoolwork foisted on him throughout his years of formal education held little interest for him, beyond the art classes. And so, eager to encourage what he did best, Mimi enrolled John at Liverpool College of Art. He started there in the autumn of 1957, as did another young student called Cynthia Powell. The previous year another, even more talented, painter named Stuart Sutcliffe had also joined the art school. Both would soon catch the eye of the adolescent Lennon.

His life revolved around music and art, with a continued interest in reading and writing. Some potential as a caricaturist and humourist was identified by his tutors. John began exploring his new world in student bedsits, smoke-filled bars and small, sweat-drizzled clubs like the Cavern on Matthew Street. Sutcliffe, with his film-star good looks and genuine artistic talent, became a soul mate – perhaps Lennon's first.

But, as Lennon swaggered towards adulthood, tragedy struck on 15 July 1958. On that day Julia visited her son at Mendips. As she hurried across Menlove Avenue for her evening bus, she was fatally struck by a car driven by an off-duty policeman, Eric Clague. Interviewed in the seventies, Lennon claimed that Clague was drunk at the wheel. Clague maintained that Julia had stepped into the road without looking and the collision was unavoidable.

The impact of Julia's death on the family was immense. On John, in particular, it was immeasurable. The 17-year-old endured her funeral with his head on Mimi's lap. He would spend the following two decades trying to come to terms with her death, his confusion, anger and grief spilling over into song, from 'Help!' (1964), to 'Julia' (1968) and 'Mother' (1970). He lost her twice, he later said; first when she willingly abandoned him to be raised by Mimi, and again when she was killed.

However, another female was soon there to fill the void. Already a precocious womaniser, John had allegedly lost his virginity with a strawberry-blonde, Barbara Baker, and notched up several conquests since, chiefly amongst the Quarrymen's willing 'groupies'. Nineteen-year-old Cynthia Powell was different. Short-sightedness was, superficially, all they had in common. The two students moved in completely different circles at art school until the day Lennon decided to sit behind the clean-cut Cynthia in lettering class. Put off by his greasy, Teddy Boy look, Cynthia initially ignored the way he teased her for her 'posh' Birkenhead accent and tweed twinset. Gradually, however, the prankster Lennon won over 'Miss Prim'. 'We never met anywhere but the lettering class,' she wrote. 'But I found myself hurrying to it, looking out for him.'[6]

Halfway through term Cynthia realised she was falling for bad-boy Lennon. 'He wasn't at all the type of boy I'd imagined myself with,' she later wrote. John brought out his guitar after class one day and strummed a version of 'Ain't She Sweet', fixing her with a steady stare throughout the rendition, and stole her heart. Cynthia was formally engaged to another, but when John eventually swept her off to Stuart Sutcliffe's room, after a night in the pub, she was happy, 'hugely happy', to be with him. 'At that moment I would have gone anywhere with him.'[7]

As their relationship developed, the naturally protective Cynthia reported tales of John's resentment, even towards her friendships with other girls, and his increasing demands for daily reassurance. Lennon was a possessive, angry teen, grappling with his closeted feelings of loss and abandonment. But when he wasn't being consumed by jealousy, the charming romantic was composing love poems on scraps of paper and slipping them into Cynthia's hands during classes. At Christmas 1958, he wrote in a card for her, 'Our first Christmas, I love you, yes, yes, yes', neatly prefiguring the lyrics to one of the first Beatles' hits, 'She Loves You'. As 1959 wore on the couple gradually became inseparable. Never one to do things by halves, the insecure John was obsessed.

His other obsession was rock 'n' roll. The Quarrymen, following several line-up changes over the previous twelve months, now featured not only the juvenile Paul McCartney but an even younger guitarist, George

Harrison, just 16. McCartney had befriended him on the school bus and recognised his precocious guitar talents. According to Bill Harry, one of his closest art school allies, Lennon was against Harrison joining the band, 'He thought he was a kid and he didn't particularly like George all that much'.[8] In 1987, Harrison responded, 'He misread me. He didn't realise who I was … [Lennon and McCartney] were so busy being John and Paul, they failed to realise who else was around at the time.'[9]

After one gig the band's drummer defected, leaving the three teen rockers lacking a rhythm section. As they cast around for someone to keep the beat, in August 1959 the trio landed a residency at a new club, the Casbah, run by Mona Best, the wife of a prominent Liverpudlian boxing promoter. It soon doubled as the Quarrymen HQ. Only John remained from the initial line-up and, now that he was at art college, the school-band association demanded a rebranding.

It wasn't just the name that needed updating. His first guitar had been a good starter, but he needed something better, something electric. 'I battled against it for some time,'[10] Aunt Mimi recalled, aware of the distraction the instrument would be from his all-important studies. Eventually, under duress, she took her nephew to a Liverpool music shop and put a down-payment on a new hollow-body Hofner. It was Mimi's tacit acknowledgement that, just maybe, John could make something after all out of his passion for music.

With Sutcliffe (who now shared a flat with Lennon) on electric bass – an instrument he could barely play –

the band, for now renamed Johnny and the Moondogs, coalesced into something more resembling a slick rock 'n' roll combo, rather than the homespun skifflers of a year or two earlier. The Moondogs morphed into the Beetles, then the Silver Beetles and the Beatals (a pun suggesting they could beat all-comers) before finally settling on the hip-sounding Beatles, in spring 1960.

The quartet still lacked a reliable drummer. This was remedied with the appointment of Pete Best, son of the Casbah's manager. The five-piece, managed by local entertainment kingpin and nightclub owner Allan Williams, were ready for anything. Williams booked them a six-week engagement in Hamburg, West Germany. The destination was the city's notorious nightclub district, centred on the Reeperbahn's red-light area and the neon-lit St Pauli district. John was excited at the prospect of performing in such exotic surroundings and immediately applied for a passport.

In the middle of August 1960, ten people – the band plus entourage – crammed into an Austin minivan and rattled down to Harwich, where they were winched on board a North Sea ferry. The plan was to drive through the Netherlands to Hamburg. They stopped en route to stretch their legs at Arnhem, where John wandered into a music shop. He wasn't averse to shoplifting, recalled Pete Best, and on this occasion he 'dipped a harmonica'.[11] Legend has it that it was this instrument which Lennon would blow on 'Love Me Do', the Beatles' first record, still two years in the future at this point. The instrument was always in Lennon's pocket, ready for action to alleviate the boredom on the road, at the urging of the band, 'Yeah, John, vamp on it, do it!'

The Beatles were scheduled to play Hamburg nightclubs managed by Bruno Koschmider. The audiences included students, prostitutes and American servicemen, all hungry for authentic rock 'n' roll. Although expecting to play at the Kaiserkeller, Koschmider's new flagship venture, the band was instead offered a slot at the Indra, a smaller backstreet venue, where they debuted on 17 August 1960, billed initially (and erroneously) as the Silver Beatles. Their run here was to last forty-eight nights, six or seven hours a night.

It was to prove the most important six weeks in the Beatles' career to date. Responding to Koschmider's demands to '*mach shau*' (in other words, 'liven it up') the band turbo-charged their stage act. Musically they improved night on night, getting tighter and stronger, while John kept the audience amused between songs by staging mock fights and generally clowning about. The crowd loved it. If nothing else, Hamburg confirmed Lennon as a consummate showman.

Eventually the Beatles grew too big for the tiny Indra and graduated to the larger Kaiserkeller Club. A week before John's twentieth birthday, in October 1960, another Liverpool band, Rory Storm and the Hurricanes, rolled into town. The Hurricanes were already well-loved back home and boasted a top drummer who would soon prove vital to the Beatles' irresistible mix of personality and musicianship: Ringo Starr.

The band's look was also coalescing in Hamburg, largely with the help of a group of artistically precocious followers who termed themselves 'Exis'. Klaus Voormann, a graphic designer, chanced upon John and the Beatles one evening as he fell into the Kaiserkeller following an argument with his girlfriend, photographer Astrid Kirchherr. 'It was like hearing every great rock 'n' roll tune there had ever been, sung by all the greatest singers,'[12] he said.

Voormann, Kirchherr and their solemn clan took all five of the Beatles under their wing, but it was John and Stu – evidently the artistic component of the band – who appeared changed as a result of their meeting. Inspired by the Exis, the band hit on the idea of adopting an edgy 'street' look of black leather jackets and obsidian Ray-Bans. It was a winning formula that added to the Beatles' attraction. John, who had developed a promiscuous appetite for sex, was even more in demand within the liberated environment of the Reeperbahn.

But behind John's popularity and his confident, cocksure front hid an unhappy man. Astrid was the first photographer to point a camera at John and reveal the lost little boy crippled inside, rather than the face-pulling wit who usually gurned back at the lens. With her lively, artistic temperament she seemed to bring out in John a gentler, more cultured side often supressed in the name of rock 'n' roll.

By the end of their tenure at the Kaiserkeller the Beatles had transformed from wide-eyed wannabes into polished – if exhausted – professionals. At the start of December 1960 John and Stuart found themselves stranded in Hamburg without work permits, the remaining band having been deported following a fire at the nightclub (the authorities also discovered that George Harrison was underage). Stuart remained with Astrid for now. John made his way back to Liverpool on borrowed money.

3

'Oh Yeah, I'll Tell You Something'
– From the Cavern to the World

I wasn't too keen on reaching twenty-one.
I remember one relative saying to me, 'From now on
it's all downhill'.

John Lennon
(*Beatles Anthology*, p.58)

Cynthia Powell was delighted to find her boyfriend back in Liverpool again. Whatever she knew, or guessed, of his unfaithful life over the previous three months – her autobiography only hints at jealousy in relation to Astrid Kirchherr – as far as she was concerned their relationship was back on track.

But the John she welcomed home was dispirited. 'After all their success they'd drifted back to England ... with no prospects and no idea of what to do next,'[13] she wrote. John had returned virtually penniless, and resuming his relationship with Cynthia caused tensions between him and Aunt Mimi.

Paul McCartney and George Harrison took on day jobs. Then, on 17 December 1960 the Beatles made their first post-Hamburg appearance at the Casbah. It was time to put all they had learned in Germany to the test on home ground. Those who saw them play, notably Cynthia, couldn't believe the transformation.

Their reputation as the hottest act in town soon spread across Liverpool and bookings came thick and fast. Pete Best's mother Mona urged the city's Cavern Club to give them a try. The Cavern was a grimy, brick-lined, triple-arched cellar: an airless, tight space originally used for storing foodstuff but now serving as a jazz venue. It had no heating (not that it was needed on a good night) and no emergency exit. The Quarrymen had once taken to its 2ft-high stage, but Lennon brought the Beatles to play there for the first time on 9 February 1961, for a prospective lunchtime residency.

McCartney, now earning a tempting regular wage as an office clerk, only showed up after Lennon threatened to kick him out of the band if he didn't take the time off work. The gig earned the leather-clad musicians £5 and was the first of 292 Beatles appearances at the now legendary venue.

Aunt Mimi continued to keep a close eye on John, even on one occasion marching down to the Cavern to see for herself what her nephew was up to. She wasn't amused. 'I gave him a piece of my mind after the show,' she recalled. 'I was mad at him because he ought to have been at the art college studying, not playing at a place like that.'[14] Perhaps it was Mimi's ever-watchful presence – now apparently invading even the inner sanctum of his Beatles world – or maybe it was his natural wanderlust – but John was nostalgic for Hamburg. He missed the freedom, the buzz and the unfettered lifestyle. As exciting as Liverpool was in 1961, his hometown failed to match with quite the same bacchanalian excess. 'I grew up in Hamburg, not Liverpool,'[15] he commented in later years.

So a return trip to the German city was arranged. Sutcliffe went on ahead; Lennon and the rest of the band arrived on 1 April. They were due to play at another Hamburg club – the Top Ten – where they were booked to share the bill with Tony Sheridan, who'd made his name as a guitarist on the *Oh Boy!* television show. When the band leader Bert Kaempfert, scouting talent for the German Polydor label, signed Sheridan, he also got the Beatles as a backing band.

John and the Beatles (erroneously credited as the Beat Brothers) accompanied Sheridan on five songs, with 'My Bonnie' cherry-picked as the single A-side. McCartney played bass for the first time. After the session – which John dismissed as 'just Tony singing ... with us banging in the background'[16] – Kaempfert was sufficiently curious to let the Beatles cut two songs of their own. John sang a version of 'Ain't She Sweet', but the one that caught the band leader's ear was a self-penned instrumental, written by John, 'Cry for a Shadow'.

Impressed he may have been, but ultimately Kaempfert did nothing with John Lennon's first recording session and the tracks were left to gather dust in the vaults until the mid-nineties when the *Anthology* project exhumed the historic tape for commercial release. It was frustrating for the ambitious Lennon who felt that the Beatles were done a disservice in the studio. He later claimed that 'our best work was never recorded'. 'What we generated was fantastic, when we played straight rock, and there was nobody to touch us in Britain.'[17] Lennon felt that once the band began recording, something of their live spirit was lost.

Back in Liverpool the Beatles garnered even more attention and plaudits, but Lennon was still unsure where he was headed. Turning 21 in October 1961, he began to feel he was past it, 'even before we'd made a record, I was thinking ... that I'd missed the boat'.[18] Many American stars were teenagers; Lennon had now reached his majority. How could he carry on playing teen music? He considered returning to art school, and sent long, rambling letters on the subject to Stuart Sutcliffe in Hamburg. News came back that Stu's enviable artistic life with Astrid was marred by ill health, notably severe headaches. By the end of the year he had quit the Beatles.

Using some birthday money, John took Paul with him for a brief holiday in Paris, to visit a Hamburg friend, Jürgen Vollmer. Impressed at the way Vollmer styled his hair, combing it forward rather than back, in the British Teddy Boy style, both Beatles decided to 'go continental' and adopt the mop-top look. Back in Liverpool, Lennon resumed the gig circuit with a new haircut and a fresh optimism.

He wrote for the local *Mersey Beat* magazine, penning an article entitled 'Being a Short Diversion on the Dubious Origins of the Beatles', 'because even back then they were asking "How did you get the name 'The Beatles'?"'. It was a humorous, scatological piece in the style of one of his heroes, Spike Milligan of the Goons radio comedy troupe, and appeared in the magazine on 6 July 1961 – four years to the day after the meeting with McCartney at Woolton fete. Answering the question, Lennon joked that 'a man appeared on a flaming pie and said unto them, "From this day on you are Beatles with an 'A'". Thank you.'[19]

The Beatles were becoming difficult to avoid in Liverpool, certainly for anyone with even the most tenuous connections to the city's entertainment industry. Brian Epstein – six years Lennon's senior and from a very different, more refined, cultural background – ran the family business, a large electrical shop which included a sizeable selection of vinyl records, catering for all tastes. Epstein's office was a stone's throw from the Cavern and the store was a natural magnet for the gaggles of record-buying youths who attended the venue's lunchtime sessions.

Epstein was acutely aware of the region's up-and-coming bands and heard about Lennon and the Beatles before hearing a note by them. Perhaps weary of the retail world he had inherited, curiosity got the better of him and he followed his teenage customers down the Cavern's stone steps to see what all the fuss was about. He was entranced. Epstein may not have understood pop music, but he looked around him at the attentive, aroused audience and realised the business potential. 'We were in a daydream till he came along,' commented the equally affected Lennon, 'We'd no idea what we were doing.'[20]

Lennon, impressed by Epstein's public school education, perceived that he might admirably represent the band in their dealings with the sort of people they would be up against if they were to make it big – lawyers, record executives, newspaper editors. Initially McCartney wasn't keen; but John was persuasive and the Beatles, after all, were his band. By the end of the year Epstein was their manager.

Although Lennon had already agreed to sign up with Epstein, he still needed his aunt's approval. Mimi was taken with the smartly dressed, well-spoken Epstein and 'flabbergasted because he told me he thought John was really talented and that [the Beatles] were going places.'[21] She had assumed the only place her wayward nephew was headed was the employment exchange.

Epstein's first achievement as the Beatles' manager was to persuade Polydor to issue Tony Sheridan's 'My Bonnie' in the UK, the backing this time correctly credited to the Beatles. More importantly, he began making noises about securing the band a recording contract of its own. Through his industry connections, a Decca producer was duly persuaded up to Liverpool to witness a performance at the Cavern.

As a consequence, 1962 began for the Beatles with an audition on New Year's Day, at Decca's north London studios. They recorded fifteen carefully selected songs based on their Cavern set, designed to showcase their versatility, but were turned down by Dick Rowe, Decca's A&R executive. As Epstein put it in a famous quotation (later denied by Rowe), 'Mr Rowe … said to me, "Not to mince words, Mr Epstein, we don't like your boys' sound. Groups of guitarists are on the way out".'[22] With hindsight, McCartney commented that he 'must be kicking himself now'. 'I hope he kicks himself to death,' came the rejoinder from Lennon. 'I listened to [the tape]. I wouldn't have turned us down on that … there weren't that many people playing music like that then.'[23]

In April came another trip to Hamburg, this time to play the Star-Club on a seven-week residency. But on arrival in Germany, John and the band were met by an ashen-faced Astrid Kirchherr and the tragic news that Stuart Sutcliffe, the man Lennon had been closest to in the band and the one on whom he depended to 'tell me the truth', had died suddenly of a cerebral haemorrhage.

The impact of Sutcliffe's death on John was enormous and terrible, and it stayed with him for the rest of his life.

As Yoko Ono later remarked, 'I felt I knew Stuart because hardly a day went by that John did not speak about him.'[24] Unable to attend his friend's Liverpool funeral due to the Beatles' engagement in Hamburg, Lennon did what he had learned to do best by 1962: hide his love away.

Despite his pride at the thrilling live sound the Beatles had hewn in Liverpool and honed in Hamburg, Lennon was, by his own admission, a 'record man' – he complained that when he witnessed Jerry Lee Lewis or Little Richard in concert, the hits they bashed out weren't the same as the versions he knew and loved. Thus, getting the Beatles onto vinyl was a priority for Lennon.

So it was with cautious enthusiasm that Epstein was greeted when he returned from one of his missions to London – during which he would knock on record company doors, only to come home empty-handed – with the announcement that he had spoken with EMI and that their producer George Martin was interested. Martin, who ran the Parlophone label, had produced records by Lennon's comic heroes, the Goons, and counted Spike Milligan and Peter Sellers as acquaintances. As far as John was concerned, he sounded perfect.

On 6 June 1962 the Beatles recorded four songs at EMI's Abbey Road Studios for possible single release. Live, the Beatles had already begun to trial their own compositions, in between the standard fare of American R&B covers. Lennon's sole contribution, the final song to be taped, was 'Ask Me Why', a lilting, soulful ballad. Martin was pleased with the results, although he asked Epstein to make one personnel change in the band. The problem was Pete Best.

John later maintained, with typical insensitivity, that the band simply needed a percussionist when they made their first trip to Germany, and Pete's face fitted. 'We were always going to dump him when we found a decent drummer,' he said. 'He looked nice and the girls liked him, so it was all right.'[25] In August 1962, Lennon asked their friend, the 'mean, moody and magnificent' Ringo Starr, to trim his beard, rearrange his hairstyle and join the band.

With Ringo on board, the four were made fab. What was not quite so fab for John was the announcement from Cynthia that she was pregnant. 'I was a bit shocked,' he later confessed. 'But I said, "Yes, we'll have to get married".'[26] He told Aunt Mimi the day before the wedding. 'I said Cyn was having a baby, we were getting married tomorrow, did she want to come?' Mimi just let out a groan. 'He wasn't ready to marry,' wrote Cynthia.[27] According to her, John's principal concern was a fear that a married frontman would be to the detriment of the band's image. Would John have wed Cynthia had she not fallen pregnant? Possibly not, although Cynthia remained adamant that they both believed they would marry one day.

On the grey, overcast morning of 23 August 1962, Cynthia put up her hair in a French pleat, slipped into a pair of black shoes, slid on some pink lipstick and, escorted by Brian Epstein, set off for the register office in her Sunday best. John wore a black suit and tie and a white shirt, the same attire he might have worn to Stuart Sutcliffe's funeral four months earlier, had he attended. As the brief ceremony got underway and John put a £10 wedding ring on Cynthia's finger, a workman outside the window began pneumatic drilling, drowning out the couple's vows. John's wedding night was spent not in some exotic honeymoon location, but across the Mersey, where the Beatles had an engagement at the Riverpark Ballroom, Chester.

Although Mimi didn't attend the wedding, she did give them houseroom at Mendips. And if she disapproved of his marriage to Cynthia, she at least approved of Epstein's attempts to smarten up her nephew. The Beatles were less popular in southern England than on home turf; their coarse, streetwise image tended to put off dancehall promoters further afield. Epstein urged them to abandon the leather for a collar and tie. The ambition in John overtook the cool. 'I'll wear a suit. I'll wear a bloody *balloon* if somebody's going to pay me. I'm not in love with the leather *that* much.'[28] Lennon's little rebellion was to keep his tie loose, with the top button undone, until Paul tidied him up. When Lennon saw them dressed in shirts and waistcoats in the first ever television footage of the Beatles – shot at the Cavern the evening before his wedding, for a slot on the Granada programme *Know the North* – he was aghast. 'It just wasn't us,' he said. 'Watching that film, I knew that that was where we started to sell out.'[29]

A fortnight after the wedding, John and the band were back at EMI Studios, this time to record 'Love Me Do', the track George Martin had selected as their first single. Lennon probably used the harmonica he had stolen in the Netherlands two years earlier, aping the riff, played by Delbert McClinton, from Bruce Channel's contemporary hit 'Hey! Baby'. John's harmonica burst gave the song a sufficiently novel tweak to get it noticed by radio DJs, who helped nudge it into the lower reaches of the British Top 20. Few record buyers, beyond their Merseyside fan base, thought much more of it – some even thought it was a humorous song, especially as it appeared on Parlophone, EMI's mostly comedy and spoken-word subsidiary.

If 'Love Me Do' packed a hidden punch, the Beatles' second single was a blatant killer. Lennon's 'Please Please Me' was recorded in the fading light of 1962 and released in the new year; it was written at Mendips by John, echoing the title of Bing Crosby's song 'Please' – and perhaps also James Brown's 1959 R&B import 'Please Please Please'. It was then given a radical overhaul in the studio at Martin's behest. 'Please Please Me' was a soundtrack to adolescent lust, swelling in an orgiastic chorus of frustrated 'come-ons'. Listeners surrendered to Lennon's excitable persuasions and blatant sexuality: pop had never known such an energetic two minutes. The hit confirmed the Beatles' potential as both performers and writers and prompted music publisher Dick James to suggest to Epstein the founding of Northern Songs, a bespoke company for the song writing partnership of Lennon–McCartney.

From now on Lennon's life would be inextricably entwined, both personally and professionally, with the Beatles. He may have felt, after witnessing his suited and booted band on television, that they had sold out to commercialism, but at the same time he must have pinched himself. Fame had been thrust upon him.

4

'Above Us Only Sky' – Beatle

I love the Beatles, I'm proud of the music.

John Lennon
(Cott, *Days That I'll Remember*, p.198)

From assassinations, missile crises and audacious train robberies to civil rights marches and political scandal, 1963 was a momentous year in contemporary history, cast in what British Prime Minister Harold Wilson termed the 'white heat of technology'. John Lennon's response was to shrug his shoulders. 'I don't suppose I think much about the future,' he told author Michael Braun at the start of the year. 'I don't really give a damn … It's selfish but I don't care too much about humanity – I'm an escapist.' Lennon admitted he had 'spasms of being intellectual' and read a bit about politics, 'but I don't think I'd vote for anyone; no message from any of those phoney politicians is coming through to me'.[30]

Of more pressing concern was getting the next Beatles record out. Cut at Abbey Road on one day – 11 February 1963 – their first long player, *Please Please Me*, was, and remains, a debut to be reckoned with. Lennon was suffering from a cold that day, but with the help of tea, cigarettes and throat pastels, he hollered and harmonised the lead on tracks such as 'Misery', 'Anna', 'Baby it's You' and his (and arguably the record's) *pièce de résistance*, a vocal-shredding cover of the Isley Brothers' US hit, 'Twist and Shout'. A month later the album was pinned to the No. 1 spot, where it stayed until dislodged that autumn by the band's second collection, *With the Beatles*.

BBC radio appearances provided the Beatles with an exposure undreamed of the previous year. In between performances they chatted with hosts in a light-hearted 'youth-friendly' style typical of the corporation in the early sixties. The format was the perfect showcase for Lennon's irreverent wit and impudent charm. 'I'm John and I too play a guitar,' he declared as the band introduced themselves, adding an impromptu 'and sometimes I play the fool'.[31] Lennon's comments in such circumstances would become more acerbic as the years progressed, but in 1963 he was only too happy to be court jester.

His front – part comedian, part tough guy – concealed many things, not least a genuinely enquiring mind. In Cambridge with the Beatles in 1963, he asked the film-maker Tony Palmer (then an undergraduate commissioned to review the gig for *Varsity* magazine) if he could show him the university. The following day, Palmer escorted the thinly-disguised Beatle around several Cambridge colleges. Lennon, away from the screaming fans, was relaxed and fascinated to see the renowned seat of learning.

Between the rush of fame and the pressure to tour and record, Lennon's personal life was compromised. He was unable to be at the Liverpool hospital with Cynthia as she gave birth to their first child – christened John Charles Julian Lennon – after a difficult 24-hour labour, on 8 April 1963. 'The worst part of the day was visiting time, when beaming husbands and relatives, bearing flowers and chocolates, turned up to sit beside every other woman in the ward,'[32] wrote Cynthia. John was in the south of

England touring with the Beatles. He wouldn't see Julian until the baby was three days old.

When he finally arrived at the hospital – in a whirlwind, according to Cynthia, and with tears in his eyes at the first sight of his son – he moved her into a private room to avoid any unwelcome attention. Behind closed doors though, he refused to change nappies, or even remain in the room when Cynthia performed the necessary chore. 'He'd bolt out,' she recalled, 'saying "God, Cyn, I don't know how you do it".'[33]

After all the turmoil and demands of the year, a vacation was in order. Lennon already had one planned, but it was not to include Cynthia and Julian. 'I wasn't going to break the holiday for a baby,' he recalled. 'I just thought what a bastard I was and went.'[34] At the end of April, he spent a week in Spain with Epstein. On their return, the Cavern DJ Bob Wooler insinuated that Lennon and Epstein were lovers. The accusation touched a raw nerve. 'I must have been frightened of the fag in me,' said Lennon later. In the heat of the moment, and drunk, he saw red and laid into Wooler. 'For the first time I thought, "I can kill this guy". I just saw it, like on a screen: if I hit him once more, that's going to be it.'[35] Lennon pulled back, fearing his own muscle. 'That's when I gave up violence, because all my life I'd been like that,' he admitted. It was, he maintained, the last proper fist-fight he ever had. Mostly his combustible temper flared up as just verbal abuse, but not always – he later confessed to hitting Cynthia. His mother's death coloured his attitude towards women: more than one account tells of tantrums and worse. 'I used to be cruel to my woman,' he said in 1980. 'I couldn't express myself and I hit. I fought men and I hit women.'[36]

True, Lennon and his manager had grown very close and it is conceivable that Epstein propositioned his charge during the holiday. 'It was my first experience with someone I knew was a homosexual,' said Lennon. 'It was almost a love affair, but not quite. It was never consummated. But we did have a pretty intense relationship.'[37]

By the end of 1963, with Beatlemania in full swing, Lennon had indeed risen to the 'toppermost of the poppermost', as he had liked to quip in the early days, when the Beatles gave themselves a pep talk about where they were headed. Not only had he performed in front of the Queen Mother and Princess Margaret at the Royal Variety Performance, televised to the nation, he'd had the gall to ask them to 'rattle their jewellery'. It was the moment Britain fell in love with Lennon the entertainer. Speaking later about the appearance, he was typically dismissive. 'That show's a bad gig anyway,' he reckoned. 'I cracked a joke on stage. I was fantastically nervous, but I wanted to say something just to rebel a bit, and that was the best I could do.'[38] Throughout his life, Lennon revelled in rebellion, or the idea of it. He was happy to be the fly in the ointment, the seditious agitator always needling away at authority.

On 7 February 1964, the Beatles made their first trip to the United States. On the plane, Lennon began to have doubts. 'I was thinking "Oh, we won't make it",'[39] he later recalled. But Epstein had done a good job preparing the ground. Hordes of chanting teenagers awaited them at

JFK Airport. They touched down in New York to a media frenzy: cameras froze their every movement; TV crews dogged them for up-to-the-minute live reports; press men scribbled down every ironic, humorous sound bite, however banal.

Crucially, with the help of Capitol Records, who (reluctantly at first) licensed Beatles records in the US, Epstein had secured a slot on CBS's primetime family favourite, *The Ed Sullivan Show*. The band performed five songs on the evening of Sunday 9 February 1964, in a live broadcast, concluding with one of Lennon and McCartney's greatest collaborations: 'I Want to Hold Your Hand'. This was written 'eyeball to eyeball',[40] at the Mayfair house of McCartney's girlfriend, Jane Asher, and taken to EMI's studios the previous October. Whether or not it was written specifically with America in mind, as Epstein claimed, it was perfect for American television. When Lennon stepped forward and bounced gently on his knees, his myopia struggling to bring the screaming girls he could hear into focus, he charmed and enthralled a nation. Boys wanted to be him; girls just wanted him. Even parents were won over – after all, all he wanted to do was hold your hand. The Beatles' appearance on *Ed Sullivan* – and their performance of this song in particular – is often seen as one of the events that defined the course of post-war American popular culture.

Lennon had finally achieved the fame he longed for. And yet, according to Cynthia, the crown was not a comfortable fit. 'John loved what was happening to the Beatles,' she wrote, 'but a part of him stood back from it and watched.'[41] Lennon resisted compromising his lifestyle for celebrity any more than he needed to, yet this was becoming increasingly difficult. Inevitably, the more success the Beatles enjoyed, the further away it took John from his domestic life with Cynthia and Julian. 'Most of the time I felt like a single parent,' Cynthia said – now, more than ever, unable to be at her husband's side in public. 'I was excluded, just as it was all happening … I was still a secret, and I hated it.'[42]

If the deception was working in Britain, it wasn't elsewhere. As each band member's name flashed up on screen during the *Ed Sullivan* broadcast, Cynthia – at John's insistence, part of the entourage that accompanied the Beatles to America – must have given a wry smile when John's appeared: it was accompanied by a caption, 'Sorry girls, he's married'. The secret was now shared with 73 million viewers across America but it made little difference.

In September 1963 the Lennon family set up home in London, renting a Knightsbridge apartment under the pseudonym Hadley. On their return there in the spring of 1964, Lennon was immediately called up for the next Beatles project. *A Hard Day's Night* was to be a single, album and movie. It was an apt title, courtesy of Ringo Starr, describing the non-stop exhaustion of touring and recording. The film gave Lennon a new medium in which to shine. Richard Lester, the director, was immediately impressed at his natural screen presence. The very detachment that Cynthia had detected in John's relationship with fame now worked for him as an actor. 'I noticed this quality he had of standing outside every situation and noting the vulnerabilities of everyone, including myself,' commented Lester. 'He was always watching.'[43]

The famous clang of the title track's opening chord heralded the Beatles' mid-sixties high point and a clutch of Lennon classics – 'A Hard Day's Night', 'I Should Have Known Better', 'If I Fell', 'Tell Me Why' – most written on the fly – made the album one of the greatest film soundtracks of all time.

The release of *A Hard Day's Night* in July 1964 followed the spring publication of Lennon's *In His Own Write*, a book of verse and short stories illustrated with his own surreal line drawings – 'a manifestation of hidden cruelties',[44] as Lennon put it. The title, like *Revolver* and *Rubber Soul*, was a simple pun of the kind that Lennon loved – 'It's a laugh a minute with John Lennon,' he commented on the publication. At a Foyles literary lunch, however, he was so nervous he could only manage an eight-word speech, 'Thank-you very much, it's been a pleasure'.[45] For once the usually loquacious wag was almost struck dumb.

In His Own Write was Lennon's first Beatles solo project and an indication of how easily he could adapt his creative output to other media. 'The writing Beatle!' hailed a sticker on first printings of the book. It was published to generally favourable reviews. *Melody Maker* declared Lennon to be 'a remarkably gifted writer' and *The Times*, whose readership hardly reflected the Beatles' primary fan base, reported that the book had even been mentioned in

Parliament, commenting that it appeared 'he had picked up pieces of Tennyson, Browning and Robert Louis Stevenson while listening with one ear to the football results on the wireless'.[46] A second volume of Lennon's writings and drawings, with the similarly punning title of *A Spaniard in the Works*, followed in 1965 and the two books were adapted for a National Theatre production in 1968.

Back home from their 1964 world tour the Lennons fled London for the leafy suburbs. John bought Kenwood, a sixteen-room mock-Tudor residence in Weybridge, Surrey. He needed some quiet time. During the filming of *A Hard Day's Night*, Lennon confessed to being 'on pills', probably amphetamines, admitting that he had started taking them when he first became a musician. It was, he said, the only way to survive Hamburg. Now he wanted to slow things down. In New York, Bob Dylan introduced him to marijuana. By the summer of 1965, Lennon claimed, he and the band were 'smoking marijuana for breakfast',[47] all glazed eyes and giggling.

In June 1965, the Beatles were included in the Queen's Birthday Honours, along with actress Violet Carson and singer Frankie Laine. It was a sign of the times that light entertainers were now given awards generally reserved for captains of industry and heroic servicemen. A few past recipients, such as RAF squadron leader Paul Pearson and former Liberal MP Hector Dupuis, were incensed, promptly returning their own medals. Although the protests would have put a smile on Lennon's face, inwardly he wrestled with the accolade. 'Taking the MBE was a sell-out for me,'[48] he later commented.

Ultimately though, Lennon had no regrets about accepting it. 'I'm glad, really,' he commented, with a more cynical seventies perspective, 'because it meant that four years later I could use it to make a gesture.'[49] He returned his award to the palace on 22 November 1969, commenting that it was in protest at Britain's support of wars in Nigeria and Vietnam – and the fact that his current Plastic Ono Band single, 'Cold Turkey', was 'slipping down the charts'.

When the MBE announcement was made back in 1965, the Beatles were at Twickenham Studios working on their second feature film, *Help!* Astute ears, hearing Lennon's title track that August, would have detected a new tone and a new theme. With few exceptions (notably 'I'm a Loser'), Lennon's compositions had hitherto fallen into the category of boy–girl songs. 'Help!' was different. It featured words not normally found on pop records – 'self-assured', 'appreciate', 'independence', 'insecure' – and was about depression, rather than love.

With emotions frayed from two years of non-stop touring and recording, the loss of Stuart Sutcliffe, his mother's death, the pressures of fame and adjusting to life as a married man and father, the Beatle-jacket buttons were beginning to lose their thread. It would take another six years of self-discovery, and the loss of manager Brian Epstein, before he could admit, with a wry grin, that 'one thing you can't hide, is when you're crippled inside'. For now, 'Help!' was Lennon learning to articulate the vocabulary of pain.

'I think everything that comes out of a song – even Paul's songs now which are apparently about nothing

– shows something about yourself,'[50] he commented in later years. His rush of late-1964 and 1965 songs, notably those for *Help!* and *Rubber Soul*, reveal the inner Lennon: 'Run for Your Life', 'You've Got to Hide Your Love Away', 'Nowhere Man', 'Norwegian Wood (This Bird Has Flown)', 'Girl'. Along with the stellar hits 'I Feel Fine', 'Ticket to Ride' and 'Day Tripper', all shimmered in a mid-sixties miasma, teetering on the threshold of psychedelia. The most autobiographical was 'In My Life', a quite different, dream-like nostalgic jaunt around the Liverpool of his youth.

Lennon was emerging as a songwriter of considerable depth and sophistication. More than that, he had become one of the most famous and recognisable men on the planet. The Beatles were, he claimed in an interview with Maureen Cleave in the London *Evening Standard* in 1966, more popular than Christ. 'Jesus was all right but his disciples were thick and ordinary,' he told Cleave. 'It's them twisting it that ruins it for me.'[51]

His provocative remarks would have unforeseen consequences. Ahead of the band's upcoming American tour, offended fans, notably in America's conservative Bible Belt, made bonfires of Beatles vinyl in protest at what they considered Lennon's sacrilegious comments. The band arrived to find radio stations had banned their records and their concerts picketed by the Ku Klux Klan. Conversely, others seemingly expected Lennon to possess healing powers. 'People kept bringing blind, crippled and deformed children into our dressing room,' he recalled. 'Go on, kiss him, maybe you'll bring back his sight …

Just touch him, maybe he'll walk again.' Faced with such extremes, Lennon remained steadfast, 'We're going to remain normal if it kills us'.[52]

But 'normal' was becoming increasingly difficult to define. At a dinner party the previous year, he and Cynthia were served coffee laced with the hallucinogenic drug LSD. It seemed to Lennon the perfect mind-bender for the self-confessed escapist. In the early months of 1966 he experimented extensively with it at home. The experience would soon filter through into such early psychedelic masterpieces as 'She Said She Said', 'Rain' and another key track of the period – 'Tomorrow Never Knows'.

Inspired also by *de rigueur* counter-cultural reading matter – notably *The Tibetan Book of the Dead* – Lennon sat in the seclusion of Kenwood and taped himself drifting into LSD-fuelled nirvana. The result was barely a song at all until shaped in the studio with the help of George Martin and his assistants. Stretching Abbey Road's four-track technology – and the patience of the studio's technicians – to the limit, the band and Martin experimented with tape effects and exotic instruments. According to the studio engineer Geoff Emerick, much of the quality of 'Tomorrow Never Knows' was down to serendipity, but there is no doubt that this track, the final one on the album *Revolver*, pushed Lennon the musician into new areas of creative expression.

In the summer of 1966, with *Revolver*'s studio wizardry effectively preventing the Beatles from playing in the live arena again, the band performed their final concert, at San Francisco's Candlestick Park. As they prepared to leave the stage that chilly August night, Lennon loitered a while, teasing the audience with the chords to 'In My Life', before finally retiring to the dressing room.

He wouldn't take to an auditorium stage again for almost three years. When he did it was for an evening of avant-garde performance at Lady Mitchell Hall in Cambridge, with fellow musicians John Tchikai and John Stevens – and Yoko Ono.

5

'Christ, You Know it Ain't Easy' – Acid, Apple and Yoko

I'd always had a fantasy about a woman who would be a beautiful, intelligent, dark-haired, high-cheek-boned, free-spirited artist ... my soul mate.

John Lennon
(*Skywriting by Word of Mouth*, p.13)

Lennon first met the conceptual artist Yoko Ono at the end of 1966, through the art collector John Dunbar. In November he attended a preview of Ono's new show at Indica, Dunbar's gallery in fashionable St James'. He arrived smartly dressed and freshly tanned from a trip to Spain. 'I went in – she didn't know who I was or anything,'[53] he recalled. Lennon liked Yoko's attitude and coolness and was intrigued by her work. A fortnight later the pair met again, at another exhibition opening. Pale, unshaven and tripping on acid, Lennon wasn't the dapper, besuited character who had impressed Ono at Indica. When McCartney began talking to her, Lennon pulled his bandmate away. 'He seemed like an angry guy ... an angry working-class guy,'[54] Ono recalled.

Cynthia became aware of Yoko when she and John noticed a newspaper article about Ono's film *Number 4*, also known as 'Bottoms'. Cynthia recalled how they both giggled at the idea of a film about people's posteriors and doubted Ono's artistic sincerity. Yet within days, to his wife's surprise, Lennon was sitting up in bed with a copy of Ono's book *Grapefruit*. Cynthia claimed Ono pursued her husband with letters and cards over the following months and had even come to the house (at John's invitation).

But for now, the woman destined to become the most important in Lennon's life, remained in the wings.

Lennon's new look – cropped hair and what would become his trademark round 'granny' glasses – were acquired in Spain that autumn, during the filming of *How I Won the War*. Lennon played Private Gripweed in the movie, directed by Richard Lester. Between shoots, at a villa in the desiccated expanse of southern Spain, he started work on a song about home. 'Strawberry Fields Forever' was named after a Woolton children's home, a landmark from Lennon's boyhood.

At his Weybridge base, Lennon explored 'Strawberry Fields' with his acoustic guitar. At Abbey Road it was pulled and pummelled every which way. Engineer Geoff Emerick experimented with backwards tapes to meet Lennon's demands, gradually adding layer upon layer of instrumentation. No other Beatles song had had more studio hours devoted to it. Finally, on Lennon's instruction, two versions, each in a different key and tempo, were skilfully spliced together to create what is generally reckoned to be a benchmark in British popular music and one of Lennon's best-loved songs. With EMI pressing them for a single ahead of the next album, 'Strawberry Fields Forever', backed with 'Penny Lane', became the Beatles' fourteenth hit.

Meanwhile, like the oils in a liquid light show, Lennon's life was slipping and sliding, morphing into an unfamiliar shape. Cynthia recalled that his daily drug taking made him disconnected, moody and unpredictable. While she kept the house running and looked after Julian, 'John was in another world'.[55]

Sessions for the next album, *Sgt Pepper's Lonely Hearts Club Band*, were underway. One song, 'Lucy in the Sky with Diamonds', which listeners assumed was a codified drug reference, was in fact inspired by Lennon's young son. 'The title was Julian's,' recalled Cynthia, 'he had come home from school with a painting of his friend.' John asked him what it was. 'It's Lucy in the sky with diamonds,' came the innocent reply, unaware the initials spelled LSD.[56]

Sgt Pepper's towering pinnacle, however, was its final track. For 'A Day in the Life', Lennon asked Martin for 'a sound like the end of the world'. Such an overwhelming crescendo had never been heard before on a pop record. 'A Day in the Life' was the sound of a band in perfect unison. The Beatles would never come together in quite the same way again.

At the album's launch party in summer 1967, Lennon appeared haggard and ill, his eyes glazed and his speech slurred, worrying many who attended, not least Cynthia. His appetite for food was now replaced with an insatiable craving for drugs and alcohol. Knowing his potential for self-destruction and his addictive personality, Cynthia feared he may kill himself. He even wrote off *Sgt Pepper* – considered by most listeners of the day, and for some years after, as the paradigmatic rock album – as sounding half-finished, 'I suppose we could have worked harder on it, but I couldn't be arsed doing any more'.[57]

Lennon's ultimate statement, however, was the song he offered up for the *Our World* TV special in June 1967, a live broadcast to twenty-four countries. Despite its lumbering time signature, 'All You Need is Love' is about as complicated as a playground chant – it mostly hops along on one note. But the lyrics neatly summed up the spirit of the times and provided Lennon with a new format in which to write: the anthem.

He nurtured his enthusiasm for innovation and was increasingly drawn to the avant-garde and ways in which the experimental could be fused with the popular. 'Strawberry Fields', *Sgt Pepper* and the Beatles B-side that ended the year, 'I Am the Walrus' (from another television spectacular, Paul's *Magical Mystery Tour*), indicated the direction of his song writing. 'I Am the Walrus' remained a personal favourite for Lennon throughout his life.

The Beatles were a global success and were defining the times in which they lived. Privately, though, Lennon was troubled. How could he make sense of what had become by now an unreal life? And how could he combat his increasing dependence on drugs? The answers came when George Harrison and his wife Pattie urged John to attend a meeting at the London Hilton attended by the Maharishi Mahesh Yogi, an Indian guru and leader of the Spiritual Regeneration Movement. What attracted Lennon was the Maharishi's claim that one could achieve a natural, transcendental high without artificial stimulants. John raved to Cynthia that 'the meditation's so simple and it's life-changing'. The following week, the Lennons, along with the rest of the Beatles and their inner circle, travelled to Bangor, Wales, for a ten-day conference run by the Maharishi. Brian Epstein said he might join them after the weekend.

At Euston Station, Cynthia, left to carry the Lennons' luggage, missed the train and had to be driven to Bangor by Neil Aspinall, the band's personal assistant. 'The incident seemed symbolic of what was happening to my marriage,' she wrote later. 'John was on the train, speeding into the future, and I was left behind.'[58]

As John and his entourage left a press conference at Bangor, a reporter told them that Brian Epstein had been found dead in his London flat. Lennon, like the rest of the band, was devastated. For six years he had been integral to the lives of the Beatles. 'I knew we were in trouble then,' he said. 'I really didn't have any misconceptions about our [in]ability to do anything other than play music and I was scared.'[59] The meditation techniques they had learned from the Maharishi helped direct Lennon and the band in the aftermath, but things would never be the same again for the Beatles.

By the end of the year, Lennon had reconnected with Yoko Ono. Julia Baird, John's half-sister, maintained that John was drawn to the same qualities he had seen in his mother, 'She was artistic, a bit fey, not mainstream, she was older'.[60] But there was also something of Aunt Mimi in there too: she knew what she wanted, as Baird put it. It was an irresistible combination. John was attracted particularly by her artistic endeavours. 'I'd get very upset about it being intellectual or … avant-garde,' he said. 'I'd like it and then I wouldn't.'[61] As an experimental artist, Ono, it has been said, was simply doing what Lennon was unable or unwilling to do.

He considered inviting her to join him on his planned trip to Rishikesh, India, where he would commune – and ultimately fall out – with the Maharishi, 'but I still wasn't sure for what reason'.[62] On his return from India in the spring of 1968, now (temporarily) drug free but ultimately disenchanted with his guru – who he concluded was a fake – Lennon admitted to his wife that he had been unfaithful to her in the past (although not with Yoko). Cynthia was only mildly shocked. She took a holiday, leaving Julian with the nanny. When she returned a week later she found her husband and Yoko Ono cross-legged together on the floor, in bath robes. John casually greeted her as if nothing was out of place. Cynthia reports that she had no idea how to react. 'The cruelty of John's betrayal was hard to absorb.'[63]

John and Yoko's intimacy was sudden, obvious and daunting. 'I've never known love like this before, and it hit me so hard I had to halt my marriage to Cyn,'[64] Lennon said. It was, he maintained, his intention to marry Yoko just as soon as their respective divorces came through (Yoko was still married to her second husband, Tony Cox). Despite his radical tendencies, Lennon was nothing if not conventional. And by the summer came the news that compounded his decision: Yoko was pregnant.

In May 1968 the Beatles launched their own company, Apple Corps, with the announcement that they were now managing their own affairs. Apple was to be more than just a record label: it would promote artistic freedom within a business model. From its Mayfair headquarters, Apple embraced everything from arts and fashion to education and electronics. Lennon revelled in the potential the new company seemed to offer, 'We want to set up a system where people who just want to make a film about anything, don't have to go on their knees in somebody's office.'[65] It was an admirable, if poorly managed, venture which attracted its share of oddballs and spectacularly failed to fulfil its initial objectives. Apple Records did, however, provide Lennon and the Beatles with a stable from which to release their output for the next decade.

The first Beatles release on the new label, issued that August, was 'Hey Jude', backed with Lennon's blistering 'Revolution'. Although the A-side was a McCartney composition, it was written about Lennon's 5-year-old son Julian, with whom McCartney had grown close. During the period of John and Cynthia's separation, he had shown the boy more attention than John had.

'Revolution' was a different beast: a biting counterblast at what Lennon considered the rebel fakery of his hippie peers. 'Ask the militant revolutionaries to show you one revolution that turned out to be what it promised,' Lennon said. 'They smash the place down then build it up, and the people who build it up … become the establishment.'[66] Clinging to the mantra that violence begets violence, and that ultimately it leads nowhere, Lennon remained the staunch peacenik. The Beatles recorded two versions of 'Revolution'. A softer, unplugged chug-along featured on their next LP, *The Beatles* (the *White Album*), in which Lennon vacillates between signing up to the revolution, or not ('count me out, in').

He also included on the album, controversially, an extended piece of *musique concrète* which he entitled 'Revolution 9'. Buried amongst the random noise of this

8-minute sound collage are snippets from earlier takes of 'Revolution'. The track was the most extreme gesture Lennon made under the banner of the Beatles and remains the most widely distributed piece of avant-garde work. 'Revolution 9' and its two parental versions epitomise the duality of late-sixties Lennon – the peace-loving experimenter and the confused rock 'n' roller, unafraid to speak from his heart. Between them, the 'Revolution' tracks provided the musical and ideological blueprint for Lennon's output over the next couple of years.

Elsewhere, the double *White Album* was crammed with Lennon classics: 'Dear Prudence', 'Glass Onion', 'Julia', 'Good Night', 'Sexy Sadie'. Earlier in 1968, two songs were recorded that had no comfortable place on any Beatle LP. 'Across the Universe', originally conceived as a single A-side, would eventually see the light of day the following year on the charity album *No One's Gonna Change Our World* (and would be resurrected for *Let It Be*). 'Hey Bulldog', thrown away on the *Yellow Submarine* soundtrack, was the great Beatles B-side that never was.

During November, complications arose with Yoko's pregnancy and she miscarried at six months. In their anguish, Lennon and Yoko immersed themselves in side projects, such as the legendary Rolling Stones film *Rock and Roll Circus*, which would not see the light of day until the nineties. For this Lennon appeared alongside Eric Clapton, Keith Richards and a yelping Ono in the supergroup Dirty Mac.

At the end of November 1968 Lennon pleaded guilty to possession of cannabis resin, following a much publicised drugs bust at Ringo's Marylebone apartment. The next day, he and Ono issued a recording they had made together that first night at Kenwood. As with almost everything Lennon seemed to be doing now, *Unfinished Music No. 1 – Two Virgins* at least had shock appeal. The cover photograph featured a self-portrait of the pair naked. 'The main hang up in the world today is hypocrisy and insecurity,' Lennon maintained, 'being ourselves is what's important.'[67] The artistically tasteful cover (shipped in a brown bag by the distributor) concealed a cacophony of tape loops and random noises, human and mechanical. The point was the gesture.

Lennon had found not only his soul mate, but his ultimate creative companion, one who would shine a light for him along the crazy paving between art and music. He and Yoko shared everything, from their bedroom to public art spaces: their first joint exhibition, *You Are Here*, was mounted at the Fraser Gallery that July. Lennon later declared that Yoko had saved his life. Eight years his senior, she quickly became the maternal partner he had so long craved.

Forces internal and external were now threatening to tear the Beatles apart. Lennon's deepening relationship with Ono meant her persistent presence in the recording studio. Sessions for the next Beatles album and movie, *Get Back*, soon dissolved into backbiting and squabbles, many of them captured on film. Recording was boosted by an unexpected Beatles appearance, on 30 January 1969, on top of the Apple building. Dismissing any last-minute doubts, it was a fur-coated Lennon who goaded his band to take to the roof and drown out the honking taxis below with a short set of new songs, including John's 'Don't Let Me Down', 'Dig a Pony' and something that dated back to his earliest writing days with McCartney, 'One After 909'. It was Lennon's last public appearance for the next few years without Yoko at his side.

Lennon's fears that, following Epstein's death, the band would be unable to manage their own affairs were proving correct. In a press interview he predicted that Apple's financial mismanagement would break them in six months. The comment attracted the attention of Allen Klein, the Rolling Stones' manager, who had also been keeping a rapacious eye on the Beatles since 1964. Not unlike Lennon, Klein grew up never knowing his parents. Coupled with his working-class credibility and fearsome business reputation, it made him man of the moment for Lennon. In the end McCartney refused to sign a management agreement, but it made no difference; the announcement that Klein would be handling the Beatles' affairs forthwith was made on 3 February 1969. 'He's even keeping tabs on me,' Lennon joked, 'He's making sure that I do it the right way.'[68] By the end of the year Klein had sliced Apple to its core, pulping unprofitable projects and personnel.

In the same week as the rooftop concert, while the band were recording 'Oh! Darling', the news hit them that Yoko's divorce had come through. 'Free at last!'[69] sang Lennon spontaneously, ending one take of the song. Two months later, John and Yoko, dressed in matching white outfits, flew from Paris to Gibraltar to marry. As an offshore

British possession, Gibraltar could grant an instant marriage licence. In line with Lennon's new reality, in which every move the couple made was to be documented and if possible turned into art, the events were related in song. 'The Ballad of John and Yoko', the Beatles' final No. 1, was the most personal of all Lennon's compositions credited to Lennon–McCartney, a writing partnership that by 1969 existed in name only. The following year Lennon revealed that they had ceased writing together 'around 1962'. All their 'best work' thereafter (surely with a few exceptions), was written separately, he claimed. 'We wrote apart always.'[70]

As the 'Ballad' recounts, they drove from Paris to the Amsterdam Hilton where, for a week, in front of an invited media the newlyweds were filmed, ridiculed and interrogated as they lounged in bed, surrounded by flowers and peace placards. Lennon, now with long hair and beard, declared the 'bed-in' to be a political demonstration of a wholly new kind, as indeed it was. 'If you want to sell peace,' he proclaimed, 'you've got to sell it like soap.'[71] Utterances between the couple recorded at the Hilton were later issued on *Wedding Album*, the third in their trilogy of experimental long players. Packaged with a reproduction of the marriage certificate and a picture of a slice of wedding cake, the album's second side included a fascinating discourse on their world view, spliced with incidental chat and an ad libbed rendition of 'Good Night' from the *White Album*. To consolidate the marriage, on 22 April Lennon renamed himself John Winston Ono Lennon. his rebirth was complete.

The Amsterdam 'Bed Peace' was swiftly followed by a similarly conceived 'Bag Peace' in Vienna and a second bed-in at the Queen Elizabeth Hotel in Montreal, Canada. Lennon later confessed that some of his earlier pacifist activities with Yoko were 'pretty naïve', but that they were simply aiming to make use of the media in order to promote peace. When asked by one journalist for a sound bite to summarise their outlandish endeavours, Lennon accidentally hit on a song title. 'All we are saying,' he replied, 'is give peace a chance.' The obvious mantra was quickly expanded into an anthem, and released under a new name: the Plastic Ono Band. A last-minute pang of self-confessed guilt (knowing he was tearing the Beatles apart), prompted John to credit McCartney as joint writer, instead of Yoko who, he said, had actually co-written it. Yoko retaliated in 1997 by removing McCartney's name when the track appeared on the *Lennon Legend* compilation (she did not, however, replace it with her own).

In May 1969, John and Yoko issued *Unfinished Music No. 2 – Life With the Lions*, the screaming/feedback track they had performed in front of a Cambridge audience two months earlier. Side two was mostly recorded in the couple's hospital room during the failed pregnancy the previous November. It featured the baby's foetal heartbeat, taped before the miscarriage, followed by two minutes' silence. On the self-indulgent 'No Bed for Beatle John', arguably Lennon's worst ever track, the pair chanted their press clippings, a cappella. The album failed to chart.

During the Ono-Lennons' peace campaigns and the fallings out over Apple, enthusiasm for the *Get Back* project that had begun in January soon dissipated and the project was postponed while the Beatles considered their future. Some onlookers accused Lennon of considering little more than his own navel. Although the tapes they had made were now discarded by the band as unsalvageable – despite the best efforts of engineer Glyn Johns – Lennon knew there was still life in the band. So when Paul proposed convening again at Abbey Road with George Martin, for what must have felt at the time like a last hurrah, Lennon agreed.

With the old formula in place, and without really trying too hard, the Beatles made their final recordings, the album eventually entitled, half-heartedly, after the studio in which it was made. Although dominated by the writing talents of McCartney and Harrison, *Abbey Road* included two Lennon classics, 'I Want You (She's So Heavy)' and 'Come Together', that gave many loyal fans renewed hope that the band's elder frontman hadn't entirely lost the plot. The last thing Lennon created with the Beatles was his lush 'Because'. It seemed a fitting end to the Beatles and the decade. Within weeks, John and Yoko were back in the studio to thrash out their second Plastic Ono Band single, 'Cold Turkey'.

Over the previous year Lennon's drug taking had led him to heroin, and he soon made a habit of it, despite it being 'not too much fun',[72] as he later put it. There seems little doubt that his addiction exacerbated his estrangement from his bandmates during the Beatles' final months. As 1969 progressed he attempted to wean himself off the drug, primarily to aid his ability to conceive a much wanted child with Yoko. 'Cold Turkey' – optimistically pitched by Lennon as a Beatles single, only to be met with a blank refusal by the other three – was a powerful document of this harrowing experience.

It was premiered with the Plastic Ono Band at the marathon Toronto Rock 'n' Roll Revival concert in September, which made it to album as *Live Peace in Toronto* (effectively the soundtrack to D.A. Pennebaker's movie of the event). Tentatively at first – 'we've never played together before' – the band ran through songs familiar to any Beatles fan – 'Money', 'Yer Blues' and 'Dizzy Miss Lizzy', before launching into the two Plastic Ono Band singles and their B-sides.

Initially, the cold turkey process seemed to be working. Yoko fell pregnant again. But the elation was not to last. On 11 October 1969 she lost the baby. This time the pregnancy lasted long enough for the birth and death to be registered – a boy, with the name John Lennon.

6

'Now I'm John' – Plastic Ono Band

I'm not interested in creating illusion. Plastic Ono was simple and straight ... that is what I'm trying to do.

John Lennon
(Sheff, *All We Are Saying*, p.88)

After Lennon's separation from Cynthia, Kenwood was put up for sale in December 1968. In May of the following year, the Ono-Lennons bought Tittenhurst Park, a Georgian mansion near Ascot, Berkshire. Tittenhurst was painted white inside and out – the couple's new favourite colour – and came with 72 acres, a lake and various cottages and outbuildings to house the retainers and, once the recording studio was assembled, visiting session players. From here John and Yoko could plot their musical, political and artistic adventures – a film season at London's Institute of Contemporary Arts; a (soon abandoned) Ontario peace festival; an Apple-financed documentary on James Hanratty, who had been hanged for murder in 1962 (Lennon adding his weight to the campaign to clear Hanratty's name). They considered virtually every worthy cause that came knocking and reflected on the decade that was ending. 'If the Beatles or the Sixties had a message, it was learn to swim,'[73] Lennon commented, urging Beatles fans to move on and, as George Harrison's Buddhist mantra had it, to be here now.

Symbolically, John and Yoko cut their hair to see in the new decade and in January 1970 they wrote, recorded and released a self-help anthem: 'Instant Karma!' left the studio and rushed up the charts just two weeks after its conception. It was produced by an old friend, Phil Spector, who had so impressed Lennon with his 'wall of sound'. As a song, it neatly echoed Lennon's push-button world of immediate gratification and his frustration with, as he saw it, humanity's failure to take responsibility for its actions. With Harrison on guitar, his Hamburg chum Klaus Voormann on bass and Alan White on drums, it was the best thing Lennon had created without the Beatles.

Spector's primary reason for being at Abbey Road Studios was, at Lennon's invitation, to examine the abandoned *Get Back* tapes they had made the previous year. The resulting album, retitled *Let It Be*, was an imperfect swansong. Many – not least McCartney – disliked Spector's lavish string arrangements that glazed the record. Lennon's 'Across the Universe', resurrected and remixed, was an unexpected inclusion and his throwaway 'Dig a Pony' was later regarded as 'garbage' by its writer. Lennon was convinced Spector had done a fine job though and *Let It Be* was issued on 8 May 1970, a month after McCartney formally announced that the Beatles had split up. By this time, Lennon was screaming.

When John was sent a copy of a book on a new self-help technique called primal scream therapy, he and Yoko eagerly read it in one sitting. Arthur Janov's theory was that the pain of psychological repression and buried feelings of inadequacy that stemmed from childhood could be released by cathartic screaming. Lennon was easily seduced by the latest fad, especially if it was non-mainstream, and so the couple wasted no time in inviting Janov over from California. 'Before, I wasn't feeling things, that's all. I was blocking the feelings,' Lennon confessed, after embarking on an intense programme under Janov's guidance. 'When the feelings come through, you cry. It's as simple as that, really.'[74]

John and Yoko concluded their treatment with Janov that summer on an American visit. While there Lennon began turning his self-therapy into songs. He worked up enough material for an album and, back in the UK, took it to Abbey Road. *John Lennon/Plastic Ono Band* stands as John's manifesto, his mission statement. 'Look at Me' was a leftover from the *White Album*. 'God' begins with a line that came out of his therapy with Janov: 'God is a concept by which we measure our pain'. The song buries everything and everyone, from the Beatles and the Bible to Jesus and Kennedy, the tempo kept at pallbearer's pace by guest drummer, Ringo Starr.

The album opens with one of the most unadorned tracks Lennon would record. From the tolling of a funeral bell, 'Mother' was, quite obviously, about Julia and the pain and anger John associated with her and her death: 'Mother, you had me, I never had you / I wanted you but you didn't want me … goodbye, goodbye'. The repetitive, half-screamed closing couplet, 'Mama Don't Go / Daddy come home' sounds like a reliving of that confused moment in Blackpool just after the war when he was asked to choose between his parents.

'Mother', on the other hand, was also his pet name for Yoko, whose companion album *Yoko Ono/Plastic Ono Band* was also recorded during the sessions, with

Lennon on guitar. With its use of floating funk grooves, free jazz inflections and ambient noise, as well as Yoko's banshee howls, it would ultimately prove just as musically influential as John's record.

Perhaps as a result of his experiences with Janov, Lennon took a brave step as his thirtieth birthday loomed in October 1970. He invited his father to Tittenhurst Park. Alf Lennon had remarried and, with his young wife Pauline, had recently had a son, John's half-brother, David (a second son, Robin, was born in 1973). John's contact with Alf had been erratic over the years but he had bought property for him in Brighton and provided a small weekly allowance. Pauline and Alf's separate accounts of the visit report that John laid into his father, telling Alf he was severing his financial support and threatening them with eviction. When it emerged that Alf was planning to make his memoirs public, John told his father he would have his body dumped at sea 'a hundred fathoms deep'[75] if he ever published anything about him without his approval. John later backed down, but the meeting was the last time he saw his father. A reconciliation of sorts, over the telephone, occurred briefly before Alfred Lennon died in 1976.

This was the ex-Beatle's angry outlaw period. He took to dressing in army fatigues or Chairman Mao cap, trademark round glasses and denim jacket, demanding to be given some truth. Gone were his vacillations over whether to be counted in or out. 'You can't take power without a struggle,'[76] he told the left-wing *Red Mole* magazine in December 1970. Back in Liverpool, Aunt

Mimi had her doubts. 'He doesn't know what he's saying! It's all an act,' she told one interviewer. 'If there were a revolution, John would be the first in the queue to run!'[77]

His views were crystallised in the fourth solo/Plastic Ono Band single, 'Power to the People', recorded on the back of the *Red Mole* interview, in which he proclaimed, 'I would like to compose songs for the revolution now'.[78] In subsequent years Lennon regretted the release, considering it a 'guilt song', written to appease the radical left.

John's bitterest bile, however, was reserved for his former bandmates, notably McCartney. Acrimony over how to divide up the Beatles' spoils would run deep for some years to come but in the summer of 1971, Lennon recorded a song destined for his next album, *Imagine*. 'How Do You Sleep?' was aimed directly at his old musical partner, dismissing everything McCartney had written since 'Yesterday'. 'I was using my resentment towards Paul to create a song,' he later commented. 'I think Paul died creatively, in a way.'[79]

Elsewhere on *Imagine*, 'Jealous Guy' was essentially a rewrite of 'Child of Nature', a reject from the *White Album* sessions. Despite John's reawakening in the years since he had first met Yoko, he was still insecure and, as he put it on another key track, 'crippled inside'.

The composition that has come to define Lennon the idealist is, of course, *Imagine*'s title track. If any of Lennon's post-Beatles' songs has transcended the hegemony of his old band, it is this. John and Yoko made a film at Tittenhurst to accompany the record's release, with John at his bleached grand piano in the music room, drenched in bright white light, the notes of the title song trickling out into bird chatter. Lennon had one of the great rock voices. Yet, despite his apparent self-assurance, especially with Yoko at his side, he lacked confidence in his singing. He asked studio engineers to saturate his vocals with a delay effect, to compensate for his insecurity. It became his defining vocal style.

Yoko, meanwhile, was also busy, with the film and album *Fly*, which featured some fine open-tuned acoustic guitar by John. Tussles between her and Tony Cox over the custody of their daughter, Kyoko – unlike Ono, a US national – drew the Lennons to New York where, in September 1971, on temporary visas, they landed with no firm departure date. The courts recommended that Kyoko be raised in America and John, tired of the racism directed at Yoko, was only too pleased to turn his back on Britain. He embraced New York City and its people, energised by its open-all-hours lifestyle and brash vitality. Yoko, meanwhile, reconnected with the New York avant-garde and set about tracking down her daughter. Their reunion would take almost three decades.

Immersing themselves in the US underground, the Ono-Lennons met various movers and shakers, from Black Panthers and Native American land rights' campaigners, to prison rioters, labour unionists and Greenwich Village refuseniks. Some of the more visible figures in American progressive politics, such as Angela Davis and John Sinclair, would become the subjects of songs on Lennon's next release, *Some Time In New York City*.

Despite its good intentions the album was a resounding flop. Nevertheless, in return, John the millionaire militant, the self-appointed 'working-class hero', was feted by America's radical elite like no other. An inevitable gaggle of chancers and opportunists washed in with the tide to exploit the former Beatle's gestures of solidarity. Lennon was at times a poor judge of character.

John and Yoko also reached out to less contentious groups, recording the seasonal anti-Vietnam War song, 'Happy Xmas (War is Over)', with the Harlem Community Choir. Its release echoed the billboards declaring 'WAR IS OVER! If You Want It', erected by the Ono-Lennons in a dozen cities around the world at Christmas 1969. It was the best example of Lennon's 'sell peace like you're selling soap' campaign style. It is also the only record on which he mentions his son Julian by name, in a whispered seasonal greeting. Cynthia claimed that John's London office sent the youngster an impersonal birthday card each year. Otherwise, Lennon had no contact with his son again until 1973.

Lennon's arrival in New York was not good timing. The United States was preparing for presidential elections. Richard Nixon's second term in office would culminate in scandal and downfall, but the 1972 campaign gave the Republicans added impetus to sniff out anyone they felt might undermine their desired outcome. Lennon, with his particular appeal to the newly voting young (the voting age had just been lowered to 18), began bleeping on the FBI radar. For almost four years, it was later revealed, he was placed under surveillance as a 'dangerous radical' with a drug conviction. His association with groups such as the Chicago Seven – counter-cultural protestors who were charged with intent to incite a riot at the 1968 Democratic National Convention – only heightened the attention of the authorities. He was under surveillance and his phone was tapped. His FBI file swelled over the years to include such 'classified' absurdities as the lyrics to songs already publically available on album sleeves.

Lennon was always careful to ensure he operated within the bounds of free speech and freedom of assembly. Ultimately, though, the authorities wanted him off American soil. Attempts to have Lennon deported provoked angry protests from writers, artists and Hollywood stars. Lawyers worked tirelessly in Lennon's defence, leaving no stone unturned, even persuading him to play a concert with his new backing band, Elephant's Memory, in aid of a children's psychiatric hospital. In the public glare, the immigration authorities backed off, but it wouldn't be until October 1975 that the New York State Supreme Court reversed the deportation order, allowing him to remain in the United States indefinitely.

Meanwhile the battle for custody of Kyoko dragged on, ostensibly keeping the Ono-Lennons in America for the foreseeable future. John returned to wrestling with addiction, commenting later that getting off methadone was much worse than kicking heroin. He nevertheless managed to contribute to *Approximately Infinite Universe* – Yoko's sprawling collection of more conventional rock, recorded at the end of 1972 – and to a couple of tracks on her final solo album of the decade, 1973's *Feeling the Space*, as well as playing on Elephant's Memory's self-titled album for Apple.

In the new year the couple moved into a twelve-room apartment in the imposing Dakota Building on 72nd Street, overlooking Central Park. Feeling that they were putting down roots at last, Tittenhurst Park was sold to Ringo Starr. Lennon would never set foot in Britain again.

7

'Whatever Gets You Thru the Night' – Lost Weekends

I'd been in many mad dreams, but this ... it was pretty wild.

John Lennon
(*Rolling Stone*, 5 June 1975)

Ensconced in the fortress-like Dakota and distanced now from the political rallying of the previous year, Lennon set about writing material for a new album. *Mind Games* – perhaps named after the tracks 'Mind Train' and 'Mind Hole' on Yoko's album *Fly* – was recorded at New York's Record Plant, with Lennon handling the production, backed by A-list session players. Released in autumn 1973, it bore echoes of the Beatles, but was firmly a seventies record, and an American one to boot. The upbeat rockers 'Tight A$' and 'Meat City' contrasted with the more reflective, and Ono-obsessed, 'Out the Blue' and 'You Are Here'. The album returned Lennon to the mainstream, making a chart hit out of the majestic title track.

Despite the public love poems to his wife which formed the backbone to *Mind Games*, all was not well on the domestic front. On election night 1972, stoked on drugs at activist Jerry Rubin's apartment, he openly seduced a female guest, in front of his wife. Ono, typically, took charge of the situation in the least expected way. She found John a lover.

May Pang, a 22-year-old former receptionist at Allen Klein's ABKCO Records, was by 1973 working as John and Yoko's personal assistant. Lennon had already confided to Yoko that he found her sexually attractive and so, to encourage her husband's infidelity, Ono approached Pang with an idea. Despite May Pang's initial protestations at the notion she start an affair with her married employer – and taken aback that the suggestion should come from his wife – she effectively had little choice. 'I was dumbfounded. I kept telling her no … but apparently her mind was made up,'[80] Pang later claimed. With the affair consummated, they left New York for Los Angeles.

Without Yoko, Lennon's thoughts retreated to carefree days when the Beatles were a struggling covers band. Arguably short on new ideas, in late 1973 he hatched a plan to record some of the songs that had inspired him as a youth. He appointed the trusted Phil Spector as producer, but Spector's erratic and unpredictable behaviour soon hampered the project. Eventually Spector fired his revolver into the studio ceiling and absconded with the recording tapes.

His marital shackles now loosened, Lennon was enjoying a new found freedom with an inebriate band of buddies, including Harry Nilsson, Keith Moon and a motley collection of Hollywood and rock hedonists. He later referred to his months spent circling LA nightspots, binging on vodka and a new drink of choice, Brandy Alexander, as his 'lost weekend',[81] after the Billy Wilder movie. It was a legendary period in Lennon's life which became emblematic of post-sixties rock and roll excess, fuelled by fame, money and drugs. But it was also born of frustration. With the oldies album in the doldrums, Lennon became restless. 'We're wasting our time here,'[82] he told Nilsson, suggesting they should put their energy into work. With Lennon producing, the pair came up with the much underrated *Pussy Cats*.

As sessions drew to a close, Lennon's past caught up with him. On 28 March 1974, Paul McCartney dropped by and in a historic cocaine-fuelled jam (with Nilsson present), the two ex-Beatles cut the last tracks they would make together, including a shambolic, widely bootlegged version of 'Stand By Me'. A reunion with McCartney, about which fans and journalists speculated right to the end, would never bear fruit. But they came close. The previous year all four Beatles had contributed to Ringo Starr's 1973 eponymous album, although Lennon and McCartney had not been under the same roof together. Lennon donated 'I'm the Greatest' to his old drummer, claiming modesty prohibited him from recording it himself.

At Christmas 1973 Cynthia and 11-year-old Julian flew over to visit. The reunion helped heal the rift between father and son, but irritated Lennon. 'You didn't allow me to be alone with [Julian] for one moment,' he wrote to her in 1976. 'You even asked me to remarry you and or give you another child for Julian's sake.'[83] Back home, Julian became the eager recipient of telephone calls, gifts and postcards from John and made three more visits to see his father while he was with May Pang.

By now addiction was running Lennon's life. 'I get my daily Yoko out of a bottle these days,'[84] he said at the time. He and Pang returned to New York and a penthouse apartment on East 52nd Street. One night, from the roof terrace, they saw a UFO. Lennon's sanity was surely being tested, but he took the sighting seriously enough to report it and include an affidavit on the sleeve of his new album, *Walls and Bridges*. It spawned two hit singles: the upbeat 'Whatever Gets You Thru the Night' and the ethereally drifting 'Number 9 Dream' (reiterating his lucky number). It also featured the pre-teen Julian Lennon playing drums on one track. It put Lennon in mind of his own childhood: the sleeve comprised coloured sketches of footballers he had drawn as a schoolboy, one bearing the number 9 on his shirt. Tellingly, the follow-up album, *Rock 'n' Roll*, would feature a photograph of his 20-year-old self, taken in Hamburg. It seems he could never escape his youth.

The previous year he had (unfairly) dismissed *Mind Games* as simply 'rock at different speeds'.[85] Although critics and customers warmed to the lyrical energy and honest enthusiasm on *Walls and Bridges*, Lennon was no bigger a fan of the new set than he had been of its predecessor. 'The only thing about it is it's new,'[86] he said on its release. In 1980 he condemned it as giving off an 'aura of misery'.[87] Nevertheless, 'Whatever Gets You Thru the Night', on which Elton John contributed keyboards, put Lennon back on the public stage.

When it unexpectedly topped the American charts, Lennon was obliged, reluctantly, to fulfil a promise he had made that if the song were a hit he would join Elton at his Thanksgiving Day concert at Madison Square Garden. Together they performed the single, plus two Beatles songs, 'Lucy in the Sky With Diamonds' and the McCartney rocker, 'I Saw Her Standing There'. It was the last time Lennon played to a paying audience. 'It was good fun,' he told waiting journalists, 'but I wouldn't like to do it for a living.'[88] Amongst the crowd at the venue was Yoko Ono. 'She came backstage and I didn't know she was there,' he told *Rolling Stone* the following month, ''cause if I'd known she was there I'd've been too nervous to go on.'[89] After the show they began dating again.

As the new year dawned, and with it a new slogan, 'Alive in '75', Lennon, now in his mid-thirties, was just pleased to have survived. 'No more 1974,' he whooped, 'I don't want to go through that again.'[90] A year and a half of suicidal tendencies and severe depression had passed in a drunken haze. His 'lost weekend' had been his cry for help.

In December 1974 the Beatles' partnership was officially dissolved and any residual differences ostensibly laid to rest. John, Paul and George met and hugged at New York's Hippopotamus Club. The following month, Lennon was tempted over to Electric Lady Studios by David Bowie for a one-day session. They tackled a cover of his 'Across the Universe' and a new song, 'Fame', inspired by Bowie's guitarist, Carlos Alomar. Despite Lennon's cursory contribution (a little 'backwards piano and "Ooh"'),[91] he received a co-writing credit on 'Fame' when both numbers appeared later that year on Bowie's album, *Young Americans*. It was, in truth, a half-hearted alliance. Lennon had other things on his mind.

After almost two years with May Pang, Lennon returned to Yoko and the Dakota. To those around them, Ono had simply kept Lennon on a very long line and was now reeling him in. 'She had the key,' recalled Pang. But Lennon was a willing participant. May had refused to exploit Lennon's insecurities. 'I didn't want to be his mother,'[92] she said. But deep down, a mother was what Lennon wanted more than anything.

The Ono-Lennons' renewed attempts to have a baby seemed an improbable mission. Yoko was 42 and had suffered several miscarriages. John had been told by doctors that he had irreparably damaged his body. But a Chinese acupuncturist advised 'no drugs, eat well, no drink'. Almost miraculously, it seemed to work – Yoko fell pregnant again in early 1975. In March they renewed their marriage vows at another colourless ceremony, this time in the Dakota's White Room.

Meanwhile Lennon fulfilled a flurry of media bookings, mostly to promote the *Rock 'n' Roll* album which had finally reached fruition when the tapes he had made the previous year with Phil Spector were recovered and tidied up for release by Apple. Notable amongst these was his last appearance before a live audience, a television tribute to media mogul Lew Grade, recorded at New York's Waldorf Astoria Hotel on 18 April 1975, for transmission that summer as *A Salute to Sir Lew*. Lennon and his band ran through two songs from *Rock 'n' Roll* and the final song he would ever perform live, 'Imagine'.

Despite the showbiz occasion, Lennon was still able to play the subversive. During the set his musicians wore masks on the backs of their heads, designed to represent Lennon's true feelings towards the 'two-faced' Grade, who in 1969 had aggressively acquired Northern Songs, and thus the Beatles' publishing rights. At the end of the show he took a curtain call dressed in floppy white cap, scarf and flares, incongruously bowing to a backing track of

'Consider Yourself' from the musical *Oliver!* The musical giant then stepped aside, unknowingly withdrawing from the public stage for ever.

As 1975 deepened, Lennon was seemingly unable to shake off the lawyers and music executives, or the ghosts of 1969. He had been sued by Morris Levy, who held the rights to Chuck Berry's 'You Can't Catch Me', claiming that Lennon's 'Come Together' was musically similar. As part of a settlement reached in 1973, Lennon agreed to record three Levy-controlled songs on his next album. But legal entanglements over the recordings, compounded by the delayed release of *Rock 'n' Roll*, resulted in Levy issuing his own version of Lennon's retro collection, comprising rough mixes of the songs. The album, available briefly by mail order in January 1975, was withdrawn from sale after three days, and Levy sued Lennon, EMI and Capitol for breach of contract. The case was not resolved until 1976.

Lennon's other legal bugbear was Allen Klein and his company ABKCO, whom the former Beatle was now keen to be rid of for good. Although the Beatles' legal problems were effectively settled in 1973 when the agreement Lennon, Starr and Harrison had signed with Klein in 1969 came to an end, ABKCO was seeking hundreds of thousands of dollars, which Klein claimed had been paid to Lennon in loans over the previous four years. 'He's suing me individually, me collectively, any version of me you can get hold of is being sued,'[93] Lennon told one interviewer.

But Lennon was quick to emphasise that amongst the many legal cases he seemed to be embroiled in, 'immigration is the important one – the others are all just money'.[94] Lennon conjured up the image of P.G. Wodehouse, as English as breakfast tea, living out his final years on Long Island. 'I'm English but I want to live here,'[95] he maintained. On 7 October 1975, New York State Supreme Court Judge Irving Kaufman finally reversed the deportation order that had been hanging over Lennon, commenting that his 'four-year battle to remain in our country is testimony to his faith in this American dream'.[96] The following year Lennon was granted his 'green card', allowing him to live in the United States. His relief was palpable.

The timing could not have been better. As the court ruling came through, Yoko went into labour. The birth was difficult and required a blood transfusion but, on John's thirty-fifth birthday, 9 October 1975, Sean Taro Ono Lennon was born.

8

'Strange Days Indeed' – Househusband

It was harder for me to stop making music than for me to continue, although I don't think continuing would have done me any good artistically.

John Lennon
(Miles, *Lennon in His Own Words*, p.118)

With the arrival of Sean, Lennon was instantly transformed into a doting father and any recording plans he may have had were put on ice. When his contract with EMI/Capitol expired in early 1976, he showed no interest in renewing it. Friends were also put on hold. Lennon now preferred to hide himself away at the Dakota, invariably leading to accusations that, back in Yoko's vice-like grip, he was losing his creative edge. 'If you can't stand the heat, you'd better get back in the shade,' jibed the critics, throwing his lyrics back at him.

Despite – or perhaps because of – his reclusive lifestyle, in the public mind there was still the tantalising possibility that Lennon might work again with his old bandmates, in particular Paul McCartney, now enjoying enviable commercial and critical success with his new band, Wings. During 1976 McCartney took to turning up at the Dakota unannounced. Sometimes Lennon would be open and friendly. At others, McCartney would be given short shrift and sent on his way, in the least polite way possible. Lennon's closest male friend, Elliot Mintz, recalled one evening at the Dakota with the two ex-Beatles, 'there came a point in the conversation … where it simply appeared at that moment that the two of them had run out of things to say … Paul said, "I guess it's time to go now".'[97]

Paul's enviable wealth had given John a nudge, though. Hearing that McCartney was worth close to $25 million, Lennon and Ono hit on a plan to increase their own stock. The arrangement was that Yoko would take care of their business interests, notably acquiring real estate, while John, by his own admission useless with money, would stay at home to bring up baby.

Lennon's last studio session for four years was to help out another old friend. During summer 1976, Ringo Starr was recording his album *Rotogravure* in Hollywood. On 12 June 1976, missing Paul and Linda McCartney by a week, John arrived to play piano on his own composition, the reggae-flavoured 'Cookin' (In the Kitchen of Love)'. The title hinted at what he was up to in New York.

One visitor to the Dakota, Klaus Voormann, was delighted to find Lennon a happy househusband, reporting that they spent all their time in the kitchen, while John baked bread and cooked rice. In between changing nappies and taking Sean for swimming lessons, the newly domesticated Lennon did daily yoga and played his recently installed juke box, crammed full of fifties vinyl. Other callers reported that the radio was permanently tuned to the easy listening station and the TV was on twenty-four hours a day. John consumed novels and books on history, religion and the occult – churning it all in typical Lennonesque style into another volume of scribbles, *Skywriting by Word of Mouth*, published posthumously in 1986.

With his residency status now secure, he could also consider travel beyond the United States. In the summer of 1977, the Ono-Lennons flew to Japan, fulfilling a long-held ambition to visit Yoko's family. John, travelling separately with Sean, stopped over in Hong Kong, where he bumped into David Bowie and Iggy Pop, who were en route to Europe. It was an incongruous meeting in the most unlikely of circumstances. Lennon repeated the Japan trip the following summer, and also visited Egypt and the Caribbean. Surely England was next on the itinerary?

A letter to his cousin Leila in 1977 suggests firm plans had indeed been made, 'We'll be in the UK around August – to see Mimi etc. – I doubt if we'll go North – maybe we'll see you in London or something?'[98] But, despite his growing preoccupation with the family he'd abandoned, he was destined never to make that journey. Julia Baird, for one, viewed Yoko as the main obstacle, blaming her for his failure to visit. Phone calls with his sisters, cousins and aunts kept him in close touch with his Liverpool clan, but Yoko kept him closer.

In New York, John and Yoko enjoyed pottering about the city. Lennon was not entirely forgotten by the outside world – when he did emerge from the Dakota he still had to brave the photographers and fans – but music was moving on. A new generation was ripping it up, much as Lennon and the Beatles had done fifteen years earlier. Lennon admitted to loving 'all this punky stuff', but was otherwise watching shadows on the wall, as he put it. Lennon, the once towering genius of popular music, was viewed by younger record buyers – when he was viewed at all – as a man haunted by the past but with little relevance to the future.

In the summer of 1980 Lennon hired a 43ft sloop, the *Megan Jaye*, and a crew, to make the 700 mile journey to Bermuda. He'd acquired a taste for the sea after purchasing a Long Island beachside house. For several hours during the voyage, Lennon wrestled at the helm single-handedly, guiding the *Megan Jaye* through the eye of a fierce storm. It was 'the most fantastic experience I've ever had',[99] he gushed afterwards, clearly invigorated at having had some control of his own fate for once.

Lennon admitted to one confidant that he had often suffered from writer's block, depression and insomnia; he feared Sean would be kidnapped, or that someone would make an attempt on his life. But the thrilling boat trip to Bermuda and the beauty of his island surroundings, miles from the New York skyline, helped him rediscover his muse and give him renewed purpose. He set up a makeshift recording studio in a house he leased on the island and cassette tapes were mailed home to Yoko.

Once back in New York, he took the demos to the studio – '(Just Like) Starting Over', 'Watching the Wheels', 'Woman', 'Beautiful Boy'. Lennon was nervous and had been out of the loop for so long he could barely remember the names of the musicians he was working with. *Double Fantasy*, his first album for five years, named after a variety of freesia he'd seen in Bermuda, was released in November 1980. He was interviewed by *Newsweek*, *Rolling Stone* and the BBC. He was now, he said, serious about life. He was back.

In the afternoon of 8 December 1980, after giving what would be his final interview, to Californian radio, Lennon stepped out of the Dakota building to a young waiting fan who asked for his autograph. Lennon obliged and a photograph of the pair was taken. When he returned home that evening, the podgy, dishevelled youth who had troubled him earlier that day was still there. Drawing a .38-calibre pistol, Mark Chapman fired at Lennon, hitting him in the back and shoulder. Lennon was rushed to Roosevelt Hospital in a police car, bleeding profusely. He was pronounced dead shortly before midnight. It was already 9 December, Liverpool time.

'I'm not afraid of death because I don't believe in it,' Lennon once commented. 'It's just getting out of one car, and into another.'[100]

9

'Through a Glass Onion' – Legacy

What [critics] want is dead heroes ... I'm not interested in being a dead f****** hero.

John Lennon
(interview given to *Rolling Stone*, 1980)

Lennon's assassination was met with an extraordinary outpouring of grief. As shock at his murder reverberated around the world, vigils were held – 20,000 convened in Liverpool, 200,000 in Central Park. No other musician's death has stirred such widespread, collective mourning. Tributes flooded in from every quarter. Even his old Liverpool art tutor, Arthur Ballard, claimed he had recognised Lennon as a genius from the start.

Lennon was compared not to that other musical giant, Elvis Presley, who had died three years earlier, but to President John F. Kennedy, gunned down in 1963, just as the Beatles were achieving fame. Both represented the hopes and aspirations of a generation. Both lives, as *The Times* put it, were destroyed 'in the quick squeeze of a trigger'.

That he had campaigned so vocally for peace made it all the more shocking to hear how his end had come with such violence. Some argued Lennon's death signified the end of the counter-culture in Western society, that the future would be somehow different without him. 'I get the sense of growing up,' commented one fan, amongst the hundreds standing vigil outside the Dakota building in the days that followed.

In the immediate aftermath, his records went straight to No. 1 and were on seemingly endless rotation at radio stations for weeks. *Double Fantasy*, rightly given lukewarm reviews by the press when it first appeared, was now hailed as a heartrending swansong and a poignant promise of what might have followed. Indeed, 1981 would have been a busy year for Lennon. There was enough material from the *Double Fantasy* sessions for a follow-up (*Milk and Honey* would eventually be released in 1984) and he was already thinking about a third comeback album. A world tour was planned for the spring, provisionally entitled 'One World, One People'.[101] The day he was killed, he had been working on a new track, Yoko's 'Walking on Thin Ice'.

Other projects were also in the offing. Ringo was the bandmate Lennon remained closest to after the Beatles' divorce. In November 1980 he had offered Ringo demos of songs written for the drummer's upcoming album. Studio time was booked for January 1981 and it also involved, separately, Paul McCartney and George Harrison, both of whom had supplied material. All three were to join Ringo in the studio. 'It's gonna be the boys!' Lennon had commented to the producer Jack Douglas.[102]

By the end of the decade Lennon's fractured relationship with McCartney had healed. Respect replaced the backbiting, despite the sometimes crackly lines of communication. Their last phone call was in the autumn of 1980, just before *Double Fantasy* was issued. 'It was just a very happy conversation about his family, my family,' Paul recalled.[103] The accepted date of their last meeting is April 1976, when Lennon busy with Sean, closed the door on McCartney, asking him to call first before just turning up at the Dakota. 'And I took that the wrong way,' said Paul. 'After that I don't think I did see him.' However, McCartney's son James, born September 1977, has said, 'I know John held me as a baby,' suggested a later meeting.[105] Lennon was certainly at home that month, embroiled in a legal dispute over newspaper serialisations of Cynthia's book, *A Twist of Lennon*.

Asked in 1982 if he had planned to work again with Lennon, McCartney replied, 'Yes. I don't know what would have happened. It had loosened up a bit.'[106] A few hours after the murder, he told one BBC broadcaster, off-air, that he and John had had plans to 'get together and to try and write music together again' and were 'hoping to meet up in the new year'.[107]

Lennon's relationship with Harrison was more strained, especially during the later seventies, although George did visit John whenever he was in New York, 'that period where he was cooking bread'. Harrison 'always got an overpowering feeling from him. Almost a feeling that he wanted to say more than he could.'[108] The rift was exacerbated in 1980 by Harrison's memoirs *I Me Mine* in which, to Lennon's chagrin, he was barely mentioned.

Lennon had the last word on a Beatles reunion, 'Anybody who thinks that if John and Paul got together with George and Ringo, the Beatles would exist, is out of their skulls,' he said in 1980.[109] The following year, Harrison (with a little help from McCartney and Ringo) released 'All Those Years Ago', a homage to John. This was followed in 1982 by McCartney's equally touching tribute, 'Here Today'. In interviews, all three ex-Beatles spoke about how much they had loved him.

Over the decades that followed, the Beatles' influence and reputation simply increased. Lennon the anti-politician, the thought-provoker, the thorn in the Establishment's side, the placard waver and anthem chanter, the songwriter and singer, continues to inspire new generations, many of whose lives have never even overlapped with his. Every detail of his life has been picked over and scrutinised. Conspiracy theories surround his death and revelations have now emerged about his long persecution by the FBI.

Like all giants perhaps, Lennon has become a commodity. His bespectacled or mop-topped face stares out from T-shirts, posters, book covers, magazines, websites and social media. Apple and Yoko have unearthed demos, alternate takes and radio broadcasts for release (notably *Menlove Ave* and the *John Lennon Anthology*). In 1995–96, two of Lennon's late-seventies home recordings – 'Free as a Bird' and 'Real Love' – were remixed by the three remaining Beatles, with producer Jeff Lynne, and issued as hit singles to promote the Beatles' *Anthology* book, CD and documentary project.

One person in particular has been responsible for the lionising of Lennon. Yoko became the natural curator of her husband's legacy. She expressed her grief in music with the release of the album *Season of Glass* (1981) and established the Strawberry Fields Memorial in Central Park. In 1988, with her help, an exhibition of Lennon's drawings was mounted in London. In the 2000s Yoko founded the John Lennon Museum in Japan and unveiled the Imagine Peace Tower memorial to her husband in

Iceland. She also edited a volume of memories by those whose paths crossed with John. In 2001, with Yoko's seal of approval, Liverpool renamed its airport in honour of its most famous son and the following year Yoko acquired Mendips, her husband's childhood home, donating the property to the National Trust.

But for most of us it is his music that remains his most public legacy, the thing that we love him for. Many of the songs he wrote with Paul McCartney, or with Yoko, or alone, will stand the test of time, as he himself knew they would, and have already been covered many times. '"Imagine" … and those Plastic Ono Band songs – they stand up to any songs that were written when I was a Beatle,' Lennon commented in 1980. 'Now, it may take you 20 or 30 years to appreciate that.'[110]

Three decades after it was recorded, 'Imagine' was voted the 'song of the millennium'. It would have amused Lennon to know that in the twenty-first century its message of optimism and idealism is still sung in primary schools across the land.

Notes

1   *Melody Maker*, 3 November 1973.
2   Mark Lewisohn, *All These Years: Volume 1 – Tune In*, 2013, p.54.
3   Hunter Davies, *The Beatles: The Authorised Biography* [1968] 2009, p.82.
4   *Rolling Stone*, 19 February 2004.
5   *The Beatles Anthology*, p.20.
6   Cynthia Lennon, *John*, 2005, p.23.
7   *Ibid.*, p.29.
8   Sean Egan (ed.), *The Mammoth Book of the Beatles*, 2009, p.519.
9   George Harrison interview, *West 57th Street* (CBS), 12 December 1987, www.youtube.com/watch?v=9xAOQS038Fg.
10 Mimi Smith interview, 1981, www.youtube.com/watch?v=LRqU2teFtw8.
11 Pete Best, *The Best Years of the Beatles*, 1996, p.37.
12 Philip Norman, *John Lennon: The Life*, 2008, p.210.
13 Lennon: *John*, p.32.
14 Mimi Smith interview, 1981.
15 *Beatles Anthology*, p.45.
16 *Ibid.*, p.59.
17 Jann S. Wenner, *Lennon Remembers*, 1971, p.20.
18 Norman, *John Lennon*, p.243.
19 Miles, *John Lennon in his Own Words*, 1980, p.35.

20 Davies, *The Beatles*, p.218.

21 Mimi Smith interview, 1981.

22 Brian Epstein, *A Cellarful of Noise*, 1964.

23 Michael Braun, *Love Me Do* [1964] 1995, p.31.

24 *Music Week*, 15 February 2012, p.1.

25 *Beatles Anthology*, p.70.

26 *Ibid.*, p.73.

27 Lennon, *John*, p.123.

28 *Beatles Anthology*, p.73.

29 *Ibid.*, p.75.

30 Braun, *Love Me Do*, p.14.

31 *Beatles, Live at the BBC*, CD, 1994.

32 Lennon, *John*, p.150.

33 *Ibid.*, p.154.

34 Norman, *John Lennon*, p.307.

35 *Beatles Anthology*, p.98.

36 David Sheff, *All We Are Saying: The Last Major Interview with John Lennon and Yoko Ono* [1981] 2000, p.182.

37 *Ibid.*

38 *Ibid.*, p.105.

39 *Rolling Stone*, 4 February 1971, www.rollingstone. com/music/news/lennon-remembers-part-two-19710204.

40 Sheff, *All We Are Saying*, p.137.

41 Lennon, *John*, p.158.

42 *Ibid.*

43 Norman, *John Lennon*, p.353.

44 Miles, *John Lennon in His Own Words*, p.48.

45 Lennon, *John*, p.190.

46 *The Times*, 20 June 1964.
47 Sheff, *All We Are Saying*, p.176.
48 *Beatles Anthology*, p.181.
49 *Ibid.*
50 *Playboy*, January 1981.
51 *London Evening Standard*, 4 March 1966, in Miles, *John Lennon in his Own Words*, p.59.
52 *Beatles Anthology*, p.143.
53 Wenner, *Lennon Remembers*, p.37.
54 Norman, *John Lennon*, p.479.
55 Lennon, *John*, p.259.
56 *Ibid.*
57 *Beatles Anthology*, p.253.
58 Lennon, *John*, pp.263–4.
59 Miles, *Lennon in His Own Words*, p.64.
60 *The Real John Lennon* documentary (Channel 4 TV), 2000.
61 Wenner, *Lennon Remembers*, p.39.
62 *Ibid.*, p.40.
63 Lennon, *John*, p.284.
64 *Beatles Anthology*, p.301.
65 Apple press conference, New York City, 14 May 1968, www.youtube.com/watch?v=nfnCTebXkhM.
66 'I Met the Walrus' interview by Jerry Levitan, 25 May 1969, www.youtube.com/watch?v=c2qX_XbsHlg.
67 Miles, *Lennon in His Own Words*, p.74.
68 *Ibid.*, p.78.
69 *Beatles Anthology 3*, CD.
70 Wenner, *Lennon Remembers*, p.26.
71 Norman, *John Lennon*, p.596.

72 Wenner, *Lennon Remembers*, p.15.

73 Sheff, *All We Are Saying*, p.129.

74 *Rolling Stone*, 21 January 1971, www.rollingstone. com/music/news/lennon-remembers-part-one-19710121.

75 Norman, *John Lennon*, pp.653–54.

76 *Red Mole*, 8 December 1970, www.youtube.com/ watch?t=293&v=huu3hPigBZw.

77 Mimi Smith interview, 1970, http://holysm0ke. tripod.com/Smith.html.

78 *Red Mole*, 8 December 1970.

79 Sheff, *All We Are Saying*, p.211.

80 May Pang, *Instamatic Karma: Photographs of John Lennon*, 2008, p.1.

81 Sheff, *All We Are Saying*, p.22.

82 *Pussy Cats* mini-documentary, www.youtube.com/ watch?v=XqkMTliizZs.

83 Hunter Davies (ed.), *The John Lennon Letters*, 2012, p.305.

84 Paul Du Noyer, *We All Shine On: The Stories Behind Every John Lennon Song 1970–80*, 1997, p.81.

85 *Melody Maker*, 3 November 1973.

86 Du Noyer, *We All Shine On*, p.82.

87 *Newsweek*, 29 September 1980.

88 Keith Badman, *The Beatles Diary Volume 2: After the Break-Up 1970–2001, 2009, p.143*

89 *Rolling Stone*, 5 June 1975.

90 Jon Wiener, *Come Together: John Lennon in His Time* 2000, p.278.

91 Interview by Andy Peebles (BBC Radio 1), 6

December 1980.

92 *Real John Lennon.*

93 *New Musical Express*, 8 March 1975.

94 *Ibid.*

95 *Ibid.*

96 *Federal Reporter*, 527 F. 2d 187, Lennon v. Immigration and Naturalization Service.

97 *John Lennon: The New York Years* (BBC Radio 4), 2015.

98 Davies, *The John Lennon Letters*, p.77.

99 Sheff, *All We Are Saying*, p.78.

100 BBC interview, 8 May 1969, www.beatlesinterviews. org/db1969.0508.beatles.html.

101 www.tpimagazine.com/Chronicle/744052/the_lost_ lennon_tour.html.

102 Jack Douglas interview (*LennoNYC*), www.pbs.org/ wnet/americanmasters/lennonyc-beyond-broadcast- episode-1-jack-douglas/1623.

103 Paul and Linda McCartney interview *Playboy*, December 1984.

104 *News Week*, 3 May 1982.

105 *Sunday Times* magazine, 1 April 2012

106 *Music Express*, April/May 1982, www. beatlesinterviews.org/db1982.0400.beatles.html.

107 Richard Skinner, in *Top Of The Pops: The Story of 1980* (BBC4 TV), 2015.

108 *Rolling Stone*, 5 November 1987, http:// thateventuality.tumblr.com/post/57672394173/ rolling-stone-interview-with-george-harrison-5.

109 *Newsweek*, 29 September 1980.

110 Sheff, *All We Are Saying*, p.73.

Timeline

1940	9 October: born at Oxford Street Maternity Hospital, Liverpool, to Julia and Alfred Lennon.
1946	After parents separate, moves to 'Mendips', to live with Aunt Mimi.
1952	Starts at Quarry Bank High School.
1956	Forms first skiffle band, the Quarrymen.
1957	6 July: the Quarrymen play Woolton fete; introduced to Paul McCartney. September: enrols at Liverpool College of Art; meets Stuart Sutcliffe and Cynthia Powell.
1958	15 July: mother killed by an off-duty policeman.
1959	August: the Quarrymen (now with McCartney and George Harrison) secure residency at the Casbah Club.
1960	The Quarrymen morph into the Beatles, with the addition of Stuart Sutcliffe and Pete Best. August: first trip to Hamburg.
1961	9 February: Beatles first appearance at the Cavern, Liverpool. April: second trip to Hamburg; first studio recording, backing Tony Sheridan ('My Bonnie'). Brian Epstein becomes manager.

1962	1 January: studio session for Decca records in London. April: final trip to Hamburg. 10 April: Sutcliffe dies of a cerebral haemorrhage. 6 June: Beatles first session with George Martin at EMI. August: Ringo Starr replaces Pete Best as the Beatles' drummer. 23 August: marries Cynthia Powell; first Beatles single 'Love Me Do' released.
1963	22 March: first Beatles album, *Please Please Me*, released in the UK. 8 April: son John Charles Julian Lennon born; Beatlemania in full swing. September: moves to London. November: *With the Beatles* released.
1964	7–22 February: first trip to the USA; appearance on *Ed Sullivan*. March: first book, *In His Own Write*, published. July: first movie, *A Hard Day's Night*, premiered and soundtrack released; moves to Weybridge, Surrey.
1965	June: receives MBE; *A Spaniard in the Works* published. July/August: *Help!* album/movie released; first experience with LSD. 15 August: the Beatles play Shea Stadium, New York City. December: *Rubber Soul* released.
1966	March: 'more popular than Jesus' interview with Maureen Cleave. August: *Revolver* released. 29 August: final live appearance with the Beatles, Candlestick Park, San Francisco. Autumn: filming of *How I Won*

the War in Spain; writes 'Strawberry Fields Forever'. November: meets Yoko Ono.

1967	February: 'Strawberry Fields Forever' released. 1 June: *Sgt Pepper* released. 25 June: 'All You Need is Love' broadcast to global millions on *Our World*. August: trip to Bangor, Wales, with the Maharishi Mahesh Yogi; Brian Epstein dies. November: 'I Am the Walrus' released.
1968	February–April 1968: trip to Rishikesh, India; begins relationship with Yoko Ono. May: launch of Apple Corps. August: 'Revolution' and *The Beatles* (*White Album*) released. November: first John & Yoko record, *Unfinished Music No. 1 – Two Virgins*, released.
1969	30 January: rooftop concert at Apple; recording of Get Back; John and Cynthia's divorce granted. February: Allen Klein becomes Beatles manager. 20 March: marries Yoko; 'Bed-in' at Amsterdam Hilton. 14 April: 'The Ballad of John and Yoko' recorded. 22 April: renames himself John Winston Ono Lennon. May: *Unfinished Music No. 2 – Life With the Lions* released; buys Tittenhurst Park. 1 June: 'Give Peace a Chance' recorded. August: final Beatles session ('Because'). September: *Abbey Road* released; Plastic Ono Band play Toronto. October: 'Cold Turkey' and *Wedding*

	Album released. 11 October: stillborn son is registered as John Lennon.
1970	January: 'Instant Karma!' released. April: McCartney announces the Beatles' break-up. 8 May: *Let It Be* released; summer: undergoes primal scream therapy. October: last meeting with father; records 'Power to the People'. December: *John Lennon/Plastic Ono Band* and *Yoko Ono/Plastic Ono Band* released.
1971	February–July: records *Imagine* and Yoko's *Fly*. March: 'Power to the People' released. September: arrives in New York on temporary visa. October: records 'Happy Xmas (War is Over)'.
1972	Immersed in various radical and counter-cultural activities, attracting the attention of the FBI. June: *Some Time in New York City* released. November: contributes to Yoko's *Approximately Infinite Universe*.
1973	February: John and Yoko move to the Dakota building, selling Tittenhurst Park to Ringo Starr. July–August: records *Mind Games*; begins affair with May Pang. October: Pang and Lennon fly to Los Angeles for 'lost weekend'. December: begins sessions with Phil Spector of 'oldies' project (*Rock 'n' Roll*).
1974	March: produces Harry Nilsson's *Pussy Cats*. 28 March: studio reunion with McCartney. Summer: returns to New York

with Pang. October: *Walls and Bridges* released. November: joins Elton John at Madison Square Garden. December: Beatles partnership officially dissolved.

1975	January: records 'Fame' and 'Across the Universe' with David Bowie; returns to Yoko at the Dakota; February: *Rock 'n' Roll* released. 18 April: final live performance filmed (*A Salute to Sir Lew*). 7 October: deportation order reversed allowing Lennon to remain in the US. 9 October: Sean Taro Ono Lennon born; first solo compilation, *Shaved Fish*, released.
1976	1 April: father, Alfred Lennon, dies. 26 July: application to remain in the US as a permanent resident approved. 12 June: final studio session for four years; recording contract expires.
1977–79	Assumes domestic responsibilities, raising Sean while Yoko works; family trips abroad.
1980	August: sails to Bermuda; begins recording again. November: *Double Fantasy* released. 8 December: murdered by Mark Chapman; world in mourning as hundreds of thousands of fans hold candlelit vigils.
1984	January: *Milk and Honey* released.
1986	October: *Skywriting by Word of Mouth* published. November: *Menlove Ave* (outtakes) and *Live in New York City* soundtrack/video released.

1988	*Imagine: John Lennon* movie/ soundtrack released.
1995–97	Beatles' *Anthology* project, including 'new' Lennon songs, 'Free as a Bird' and 'Real Love'.
1998	*John Lennon Anthology* and *Wonsaponatime* (demos/outtakes) released.
2004	*Acoustic* (demos/live/home recordings) released.
2000s	John Lennon Museum founded in Japan; Imagine Peace Tower memorial unveiled in Iceland; Liverpool airport renamed in his honour; 'Mendips' donated to the National Trust.

Web Links

There are innumerable websites about John Lennon and the Beatles, the most valuable of which include audio streams and transcripts of interviews with him and those who knew him:

beatlesarchive.net
beatlesbible.com
beatlesinterviews.org
imaginepeace.com
johnlennon.com
yopob.com

Finally, for the music itself, Wikipedia has an excellent discography, as has the meticulously detailed book by Madinger and Raile, Lennonology (see 'Further Reading').

Further Reading and Viewing

Badman, Keith, *The Beatles: The Dream is Over* (Omnibus, 2002).
—— *The Beatles Diary Volume 2: After The Break-Up 1970–2001* (Omnibus, 2009).
Baird, Julia, *Imagine This: Growing Up With My Brother John Lennon* (Hodder, 2007).
—— with G. Giuliano, *John Lennon: My Brother* (Grafton, 1988).
The Beatles Anthology (Cassell/Weidenfeld & Nicolson, 2000).
Best, Pete, *The Best Years of the Beatles* (Headline, 1996).
Braun, Michael, *Love Me Do* (Penguin, 1964).
Cott, Jonathan, *Days That I'll Remember: Spending Time with John Lennon and Yoko Ono* (Doubleday, 2013).
Davies, Hunter, *The Beatles: The Authorised Biography* (Ebury, [1968] 2009).
—— (ed.), *The John Lennon Letters* (W&N, 2012).
Du Noyer, Paul, *We All Shine On: The Stories Behind Every John Lennon Song 1970–80* (Carlton, 1997).
Egan, Sean (ed.), *The Mammoth Book of the Beatles* (Robinson, 2009).
Emerick, Geoff, *Here, There and Everywhere: My Life Recording the Music of the Beatles* (Gotham House, 2006).
Epstein, Brian, *A Cellarful of Noise* (Byron Press, 1964).
Lennon, Cynthia, *John* (Hodder & Stoughton, 2005).

—— *A Twist of Lennon* (Star Books, 1978).

Lennon, John, *In His Own Write* (Cape, 1964).

—— *A Spaniard in the Works* (Cape, 1965).

—— *Skywriting by Word of Mouth* (Harper & Row, 1986).

Lewisohn, Mark, *The Complete Beatles Chronology* (Hamlyn, 1992).

—— *All These Years: Volume 1 – Tune In* (Little Brown, 2013).

Macdonald, Ian, *Revolution in the Head: The Beatles Records and the Sixties* (4th Estate, [1994] 1997).

Madinger, C. and Raile, Scott, *Lennonology: Strange Days Indeed – A Scrapbook of Madness* (Open Your Book/ Burning Shed).

Martin, George, *Summer of Love: The Making of Sgt Pepper* (Macmillan, 1994).

Miles (ed.), *John Lennon in His Own Words* (Omnibus, 1980).

Norman, Philip, *John Lennon: The Life* (HarperCollins, 2008).

Ono, Yoko, *John Lennon: Summer of 1980* (Perigee, 1983).

——Memories of John Lennon (Harper Collins, 2006).

Pang, May, *Instamatic Karma: Photographs of John Lennon* (St Martin's Press, 2008).

Saimaur, Nishi F., *The John Lennon Family Album* (Crawford House, 1990).

Sawyers, June Skinner (ed.), Read the Beatles (Penguin, 2006).

Sheff, David, *All We Are Saying: The Last Major Interview with John Lennon and Yoko Ono* (the *Playboy* interview) (St Martin's Press, [1981] 2000).

Wenner, Jann S., *Lennon Remembers* (Verso, [1971] 2000).
Wiener, Jon, *Come Together: John Lennon in His Time* 2nd
edition (Faber & Faber, [1984] 2000).

Lennon's last public performance, *A Salute to Sir Lew*, filmed on 18 April 1975, is at tinyurl.com/pahy4t8; and his final television interview, recorded ten days earlier on *The Tomorrow Show*, is at tinyurl.com/nvxxpsj. Otherwise, I found the following films and documentaries most useful:

All My Loving, dir. Tony Palmer, 1968 (DVD, 2007).
The Beatles Anthology, dir. Geoff Wonfor and Bob Smeaton, 1996 (DVD, 2003).
Imagine, dir. Steve Gebhardt, John Lennon and Yoko Ono, 1972 (tinyurl.com/o3wpchd).
John Lennon: Imagine, dir. Andrew Solt, 1988 (DVD, 2005).
LennoNYC, dir. Michael Epstein, 2010 (DVD, 2010).
The Real John Lennon, dir. Richard Denton, 2000 (tinyurl.com/prqmmv5).
Sweet Toronto, dir. D. A. Pennebaker, 1969 (DVD, 2008).

Giuseppe Verdi Henry V **Brunel** Pope John Paul II **Jane Austen** Sigmund Freud **Abraham Lincoln** Robert the Bruce **Charles Darwin** Buddha **Elizabeth I** Horatio Nelson **Wellington** Hannibal & Scipio **Jesus** Joan of Arc **Anne Frank** Alfred the Great **King Arthur** Henry Ford **Nelson Mandela** Edward Jenner **Napoleon Bonaparte** Isaac Newton **Albert Einstein** John Lennon **Elizabeth II**